Men's Involvement in Gender and Development Policy and Practice: Beyond Rhetoric

First published by Oxfam GB in 2001

© Oxfam GB 2001

ISBN 0 85598 466 X

A catalogue record for this publication is available from the British Library.

Available from Bournemouth English Book Centre, PO Box 1496, Parkstone, Dorset, BH12 3YD, UK
tel: +44 (0)1202 712933; fax: +44 (0)1202 712930; email: oxfam@bebc.co.uk

and from the following agents:
USA: Stylus Publishing LLC, PO Box 605, Herndon, VA 20172-0605, USA
tel: +1 (0)703 661 1581; fax: +1 (0)703 661 1547; email: styluspub@aol.com

Southern Africa: David Philip Publishers, PO Box 23408, Claremont 7735, South Africa
tel: +27 (0)21 674 4136; fax: +27 (0)21 674 3358; email: orders@dpp.co.za

For details of local agents and representatives in other countries, consult our website:
http://www.oxfam.org.uk/publications.html
or contact Oxfam Publishing, 274 Banbury Road, Oxford OX2 7DZ, UK
tel. +44 (0)1865 311 311; fax +44 (0)1865 312 600; email publish@oxfam.org.uk

Printed by Oxfam Print Unit

Oxfam GB is a registered charity, no. 202 918, and is a member of Oxfam International.

Contents

Introduction

Caroline Sweetman

The papers published in this volume are a selection of the contributions that were presented at a seminar entitled 'Beyond Rhetoric: Male Involvement in Gender and Development Policy and Practice', which was held at Queen Elizabeth House, University of Oxford, UK, from 9 to 10 June 2000. The seminar was convened by Oxfam GB, with the Centre for Cross-Cultural Research on Women, Queen Elizabeth House. It was the fifth and final seminar in a series entitled 'Men, Masculinities, and Gender Relations in Development' which had begun in September 1998. The series was instigated by the University of Bradford, the University of East Anglia, and Oxfam GB, and was sponsored by the Economic and Social Research Council (ESRC) of Great Britain.

Oxfam GB began publishing on the topic of on men and masculinity in 1997, with the publication of an issue of its international journal, *Gender and Development*. As editor of the journal, I was motivated to commission this issue because I had been interested in the topic since working and living in Lesotho, where changing patterns of male and female income-generation make it very obvious that 'gender' is not solely an issue for women.[1] Over the past decade, Oxfam GB has, like some other international development agencies, placed increasing emphasis on assessing how, when, and where it should be working to address men's gender issues, in the interests of fulfilling its organisational mandate to relieve poverty and suffering.

Global statistics continue to show that women are disproportionately poorer than men, and their political and social marginalisation has not ended anywhere in the world. However, the insights that gender analyses can offer need to be applied much more consciously and rigorously to relations between women and men, and to men's own experience. Research from many different areas of the world — in both North and South — confirms that men, as well as women, are being impoverished by an unjust and unsustainable economic model. Gender analysis offers a key to understanding

that 'male exclusion' and 'feminisation of employment' are in fact two sides of the same coin. Notions of 'men's work' and 'women's work', and conventional assumptions about masculinity and femininity, are manipulated by businesses and industry to ensure a cheap and malleable workforce.

For the past twenty years, studies by feminist economists have shown how manufacturing and service sectors exploit conventional assumptions about men's and women's roles to pay women 'pin-money' instead of a living wage. The 'justification' for paying women low wages is that they and their children are supported by male breadwinners; but in reality, many of the women and girls who have taken jobs in export-processing zones and call-centres over the past decades are breadwinners themselves, desperate to support their families. Meanwhile, narrow notions of men's work and male pride and status lead many men who are laid off from heavy industry to simply give up. (An exception is men from minority or migrant communities, whose desperation often forces them to perform menial jobs often assumed to be women's work, in European and North American cities.) The result of this process is a global system where profits are maximised for owners and share-holders of businesses; the families of workers exist on poverty-line wages; exhausted, predominantly female carers are being pressured into a double day; and most 'excluded' men do not assist their working partners by taking over the housework and childcare. In such contexts of crisis and social dislocation, women all too often pay the ultimate, appalling price for men's frustration and loss of status, in terms of domestic violence and abuse. This analysis clearly demonstrates the link between anti-poverty strategies and feminist agendas.

The papers published here from the final seminar explore the ways in which development organisations have addressed gender and development in the past, the problems that they have faced, and possible ways of working which will take account of the concerns indicated above. The presenters of papers at the final seminar were invited to respond to one or both of two key questions:

- In what sectors and contexts should gender and development work involve men as beneficiaries?
- What issues face men who work in activities which have a commitment to gender equality and/or a feminist perspective?

The final seminar opened with a paper from **Anne Coles**, concerning the approach to gender issues adopted by the UK Department for International Development (DFID). She characterised men's and women's approaches to working on gender issues. She was followed by **Professor Ibrahim Shao** of the University of Tanzania, on his experience of promoting gender equality in a Southern research institution. In the panel which followed, entitled 'Linking personal commitment to organisational policy', **Chris Roche** of Oxfam GB argued that, despite debates on institutionalising gender equity in recent years, gender and development policy makers have an imperfect understanding of the issues facing men who work to promote gender equality in development organisations. What makes men want to work to promote gender equality? Is it altruism, or do they have something to gain?

As a whole, the seminar series was numerically dominated by contributions from women, and the final event was no exception. Several men expressed their regret that the current debates on men and masculinity within development research and policy seem at the moment to be dominated by women. This reflects the fact that gender issues, understood to be issues of unequal power between women and men, have been addressed mainly by women. In his paper, Feleke Tadele, also of Oxfam GB, discussed his experience of working as a 'gender lead' for Oxfam in its programme in Ethiopia. **Feleke Tadele** was concerned about how to support male social pioneers of gender equality, and about the need to go slowly in challenging cultural practices and assumptions. Many of the tensions generated by the question of who should work on anti-racism are replicated in connection with gender-related initiatives. Much work remains to be done if we are to deepen our understanding of the ways in which personal location and identity enable individuals to work — or prevent them from working — on particular issues of inequality.

Specialists in gender and organisational change need to deepen their analysis of the ways in which gender identity affects our effectiveness as professionals, and to learn from pioneers of change, both women and men.

In the afternoon of the first day, a panel of speakers discussed the issue of 'Gender Training and Men'. Gender training has been seen as a key — often, as *the* key — to effecting changes in gender relations in grassroots communities and in development organisations themselves. In her paper, **Kamla Bhasin** of the FAO discussed her technique of demonstrating to the senior male policy-makers whom she trains that qualities that are conventionally associated with either women or men are far from being associated with one sex only. She argued that, rather than seeing gender and development as the particular concern of specialist researchers and activists, it is the only sane way of understanding our world, where both women and men are disadvantaged by unsustainable development models which manipulate conventional notions of masculinity and femininity to ensure the continuing oppression of poor people, the South, and the environment. **Milton Obote Joshua**, a trainer and academic from Egerton University, Kenya, described his experience of breaking down men's resistance to ideas of gender equality through training in grassroots communities.

Day Two of the seminar opened with a panel on 'Development Policy, Masculinity, Sexuality, and Violence'. **Saraswati Raju**, from the Centre for Study of Regional Development, Jawaharlal Nehru University, New Delhi, gave a paper on her findings on male sexuality and their policy implications for reproductive health programmes in India. Both she and **Nadia Wassef**, author of the paper that followed — on male involvement in perpetuating and challenging the practice of female genital mutilation in Egypt — saw men's involvement in programmes to assert women's reproductive rights as key to the programmes' success. They emphasised the cost to men of attempting to live in accordance with a model of masculinity which is predicated on controlling women's bodies.

Two workshops followed the presentations, and the proceedings have been written up as papers for this book. **Shibesh Regmi**, of New ERA in Nepal, and **Ben Fawcett** of the University of Southampton, presented a workshop on 'Mainstreaming Gender into Technical Projects', focusing on Shibesh's research on water projects in Nepal. For those who had worked on gender issues in development organisations, the marginalisation of women from the planning and implementation of water projects was familiar and depressing. The question is how to integrate a social analysis into projects which are dominated by technicians, in sectors which are traditionally gendered 'male'.

The other workshop addressed the topic of 'Tackling Male Exclusion in Post-industrialised Settings: Lessons from the UK'. The theme was presented by **Sue Smith**, **Judith Robertson**, and **Julie Jarman**, all of Oxfam GB. This workshop echoed the previous day's discussions of male exclusion and impoverishment, emphasising the toll on women and children of men's frustration as patterns of employment change from male-gendered heavy jobs to light industry and services, where women take 'flexible' jobs. Development policy makers who aim to influence international economic policy should advocate the need for global economic and social policies that meet the needs of women, men, and children for sufficient money and time to support and nurture themselves and their dependants. Both women and men need support to fight for a decent livelihood, through challenging traditional assumptions of what work they 'should' do as women or men, in the workplace and at home.

The final panel on Day Two examined 'Men's Role in the Family: Implications for Policy'. Carrying forward the issues first raised about masculinity and sexuality earlier in the day, **Peter Sternberg** delivered a paper based on his field work in Nicaragua, entitled 'Challenging machismo to promote sexual and reproductive health: the experience of a Nicaraguan NGO, CISAS'. **Sandy Ruxton** ended the seminar with a paper that focused on the failure of the State in the UK to recognise men's rights and roles as fathers, and to promote them as carers as well as economic providers. The assumption that women are primary carers means that fathers are marginalised from their families by service providers and employers. This paper echoed a debate that had been a continuing feature of the ESRC seminar series, about the need to recognise and promote men as carers as well as economic providers. Development organisations are as guilty as other employers of demanding that their workforce work long hours that are incompatible with their personal and social responsibilities. Hardly anyone — male or female — is nowadays supported by the labour of a stay-at-home spouse, yet employment policy has still not acknowledged this fact.

No development organisation with a gender policy can ignore the challenge to evolve family-friendly policies and equalise the gender-linked division of labour. The unpaid work of caring for children, older people, and disabled people, cooking, cleaning, and all the other household tasks — which is mostly performed by females of all ages — is still largely ignored (despite recent efforts to 'value' it by counting it in national accounts). If development campaigning and advocacy on economic growth conceptualises women's unpaid work only as a 'constraint' on their formal employment, we are ignoring the need of the human race to — literally — 'reproduce' itself, and men's need and right to shoulder part of this burden. There is a challenge here, too, for project planners. The vast majority of development projects promote women's participation without providing childcare, or challenging men in the community to do household work.

In summary, the seminar reconfirmed the commitment of development policy makers and practitioners to integrate the aim of promoting gender equality into their work. It reconfirmed the need for a more mature understanding of how conventional assumptions about gender differ from individuals' lived reality, and how they are used by the powerful to exploit women and men who live in poverty. Global economic and social policies are needed to meet the basic needs of women, men, and children for sufficient money and time to support and nurture themselves and their dependants. Both women and men in poverty need support to fight for a decent livelihood for themselves and their families, through challenging traditional notions of what work they 'should' do as women or men, in the workplace and at home. The seminar confirmed that the debates about men and masculinity need to stimulate development agencies to put gender and development theory into practice: we need to practise as we preach, and focus on challenging unequal power relations directly. This means working with, and for, men as well as women.

Note

1   I discuss this further in my own article, published in this collection, which was delivered not at the fifth seminar but at the first one, in September 1998 at the University of Bradford. However, it appears here because it seems to fit most clearly with the policy- and practice-related concerns of the fifth.

Men, women, and organisational culture: perspectives from donors

Anne Coles

For many gender advocates, progress towards gender equality and gender mainstreaming since the UN Fourth Conference on Women in Beijing in 1995 has proved disappointingly slow. This paper proposes one strategy to help further progress: namely to involve more men as gender specialists in bilateral development organisations and to involve them fully in mainstreaming processes. The aim of the paper is to highlight the need for both men and women in donor organisations to be fully involved in advancing the position of women, if development goals are to be reached. It begins by looking at the progress that has been made in promoting gender equality in the work of bilateral development organisations since Beijing. I consider the special case of the way in which gender has been mainstreamed in the British government's Department of International Development (DFID). I then examine the respective advantages and disadvantages of men and women taking lead responsibility for gender issues. And I conclude with suggestions for the future.

I am basically drawing on experiences of DFID and on the recent research that I have been undertaking as an associate at the Centre for Cross-Cultural Research on Women at Queen Elizabeth House in the University of Oxford. I want to acknowledge the help of both men and women gender specialists, working at policy, programme, and project levels, who generously shared their views with me.[1]

The context

In 1996 the Development Assistance Committee (DAC) of the OECD published an important strategy document: 'Shaping the 21st Century: The Contribution of Development Co-operation'. The document selects targets for the bilateral donor community to aim for by 2015: halving the number of those living in extreme poverty; universal primary education; reducing infant mortality by two-thirds; reducing maternal mortality by three-quarters; universal access to

family-planning methods; and reversal of trends in the loss of natural resources. The indicator (or proxy measurement) for the empowerment of women is a limited though critically important one: to eliminate gender disparity in primary and secondary education. The transformation in gender relations and the gendered re-distribution of resources needed to achieve these targets seem initially to have passed largely unnoticed. But they present an enormous challenge to the development community as a whole.

Progress since Beijing

I have recently been helping to review how the countries that are members of the OECD's DAC have implemented their 1995 policy statement on gender equality, which was a contribution to the Beijing process.[2] All members have made progress, but the advance has been uneven, both across organisations and across the nine goals of the Statement. It has varied according to the 'baseline' positions of the development organisations concerned, the flexibility of their institutional structures, their priorities, and the total resources available. In no development organisation, either ministry, government department, or agency, has the strategy of gender mainstreaming been fully established, and none has reached all the goals. Advancing gender equality is proving to be a much slower process than many originally expected. Much remains to be done; and it can only be done, I suggest, by involving men much more fully than hitherto.

The adoption of a mainstreaming strategy involves taking gender considerations into account throughout the work of the organisation concerned. From this it follows that advancing gender equality becomes the responsibility of all staff — men, who are usually in the majority, as well as women. This is very different from the earlier Women in Development (WID) approach, which typically found expression in small female-staffed gender

4

cells devoted to projects on women's issues. Indeed it was because of the limitations of these units as agents for change, and their marginalisation, that gender-mainstreaming strategies have been adopted in a majority of donor organisations. Gender units are still needed to act as advocates and catalysts, to lead on policy, to provide expertise, and to support technical departments. But in order to gain the commitment of a much wider body of professional and administrative staff, both men and women gender specialists are needed.

Preliminary remarks

Any consideration of the effectiveness of men and women in championing gender policies must take institutional aspects into account, including the following.

- The culture of the development agency in which they work is critical: its mandate, which determines how gender policies will 'fit', its norms and values, its formal structures, and (especially important) its informal working behaviours, which may be very powerful. The extent to which the organisation is directed by parliament varies, but the political agenda can be important. For example, there were powerful statements in Scandinavian parliaments following the Beijing conference, and in Britain the Labour government's 1997 White Paper (official policy document) on aid, 'Eliminating World Poverty: A Challenge for the 21st Century', has had a major influence in DFID. Organisations are also variously vulnerable to other external pressures, such as lobbying by civil-society groups.
- Those working overseas need to take account of the structure of local society, the nature of partner organisations, the leading personalities and, at the level of the field, the culture of the population to be reached.

Gender is, of course, only one aspect of a person's identity. Other aspects such as ethnicity and class are also important, and gender cuts across them, often in complex ways.

- Being 'part of the modern world', affluent, or a foreigner may be more important factors than gender in the conceptual gaps that exist between the development professional and the target beneficiaries.

- Age can be critical. Both men and women working on gender equality need to hold senior positions in their organisations in order to be taken seriously. They often are neither. Young unmarried women, both expatriates and nationals, may be at a particular disadvantage in some countries, for they lack the status of an older woman who is assumed, rightly or wrongly, to be married with children. Unfortunately many development agencies lack older women staff.

Social and gender advice in DFID

The Department for International Development, formerly the Overseas Development Administration (ODA), has always had a unique structure for addressing gender issues. The responsibility has lain with the Social Development Department (SDD), which, along with the economists and the environmentalists, has formed the cross-cutting advisory cadres that contribute to the design and implementation of all programmes and projects. The agency never passed through a completely typical WID phase, although a comprehensive policy, an action plan, and arrangements for monitoring were set in place in 1987/88. There was never a separate budget for women's projects — only in the last few years has SDD had funds for applied and operational research on gender matters. The numbers of men and women who are SD advisers have always been roughly equal, potentially enabling the strengths and weaknesses of each in relation to implementing gender policies to be revealed. Most SD advisers have a research background in anthropology or social policy: gender analyses are incorporated into (and sometimes buried in!) broader social analyses. The approach to gender training for staff in general has been to emphasise the understanding and skills required for working purposes. Personal aspects have been deliberately set aside, and the link with internal equal-opportunities policies is not made.

DFID understands that if, following gender analysis, men and boys are shown to be disadvantaged, in some circumstances there should be projects or project components addressing their specific needs. This has occurred in education and health sectors particularly. Support has also been given to initiatives such as men's groups opposed to violence. Even in Bangladesh, where there is an overwhelming need to advance the position of women, a very few activities related to HIV/AIDS, health, and legal literacy specifically target men.

Bilateral development organisations are largely male, middle class, and white — or rather the institutional culture has tended to display these characteristics. Most are bureaucracies. Comparatively few welcome transformational agendas: conformity is the norm. DFID has usually been no exception. But changes are taking place, many in the wake of the 1997 White Paper. Others are the result of the growing numbers of young women who are joining DFID and who are now well established in administration and in many of the professional departments, particularly economics, health, and education.

Nevertheless, the higher echelons of the office have always been dominated by men, despite the fact that the ministers have often been women. There is only one woman in the senior directors' group, and only one woman head of profession. Key meetings (such as the board that endorses new projects) typically avoid mentioning gender aspects in their summing up. And their abrupt, hierarchical style requires considerable adaptability on the part of a woman if she is to contribute effectively in them. (Conversely, the senior development adviser — a man — who represents DFID at the DAC Working Party for Gender Equality initially found its co-operative and more discursive meetings equally strange and confusing.)

The Social Development Department has been one of the fastest-growing departments in DFID, and there has been steady progress in tackling gender inequalities. Recently the proportion of DFID spending aimed at promoting gender equality has more than doubled, from 23 per cent in 1994 to 46 per cent in 1998-99. Nevertheless, there is a legacy of seeing gender and even social development more generally as a 'soft' and second-class policy area. The 'hard' technical departments appear to be more highly valued.

The economists have a particular status and, as in many other agencies, the World Bank has a special aura of power. If, as seems likely, the Bank places greater emphasis on gender equality and supports this with 'hard evidence' from practical research, the issue will receive much more serious attention in many bilateral organisations.

There is an inter-relationship between an organisation's internal culture and its ability to deliver its external services or products. This has been clear in DFID. Thus, the introduction of team-working (from about 1993) interacted with the growing interest in process and participation in projects and programmes. The former benefited women staff, who preferred this more collegiate, verbal style of working to that of the formal written memorandum. The latter assisted the development of local partnerships for gender-specific activities in the post-Beijing era. For example, it has become easier to discuss matters such as simplifying procedures to fund NGO activities. The approach taken in DFID has been to integrate gender policies within the existing organisational structure, but senior social-development advisers have been quick to seize opportunities for transformation.

Let us now consider the respective merits of men and women in promoting gender equality in development aid. The next two sections reflect the views of men and some of their women colleagues who are working professionally as social development and gender specialists.[3] The discussion focuses on the operational practicalities of the 'here and now', but it encompasses both short-term initiatives and the longer-term objective of transforming the development agenda.

Advantages and disadvantages of men taking forward the gender-equality agenda

Policy dialogue

Given the present circumstances, a man is often in a good position to influence other men, whether agency colleagues or partners. Men's influence on men should not be underestimated: men listen to men more readily than they listen to women. As we have noted, women may have real difficulty in making their voices heard in high-level negotiations, for reasons that include problems of audibility, cultural 'invisibility', and inability to intervene in a male discourse with appropriate language and style.

A man may therefore have greater access to officials at the policy and programme levels, both at home and overseas. In most partner countries, decision-makers, whether in government, the private sector, or civil society, are overwhelmingly likely to be men. Even at project level, the 'case for women' can sometimes be better communicated by a man, especially when dealing with traditional leaders and local bureaucrats. Men cannot so easily ignore gender issues or dismiss them as 'feminist rhetoric' when they are proposed by other men.

Mainstreaming

Stereotypes still exist in many aid organisations. A man working on gender issues may be perceived as more professional and more 'objective' than a woman. However wrongly, women gender experts are often seen by male staff to be 'difficult' or 'threatening'. As one woman official put it, she and her colleagues were apt to be regarded as 'both extreme feminists and sort of fluffy'! In present circumstances, therefore, men can add prestige and weight to gender-equality work.

Involvement of men specialists can therefore help to make gender concerns more integral to the development process, more 'normal', and more pragmatic. If gender is seen only as a 'wimmin's' issue championed by feminists, it may be treated as a minority interest, as so often in the past. It may be particularly helpful to use men to champion gender issues in strongly male technical departments such as engineering, particularly where the man concerned comes from the same professional background.

Gender analysis

Men have a potentially important role to play in contributing to balanced gender analyses. Despite advances in the last few years, most gender specialists have limited understanding of male values and masculine perspectives, and of how to incorporate them into their work. There are several strands to this. Firstly it is through thorough gender analysis that it is possible to identify certain circumstances where men may be the most affected. For example, men may become severely demoralised in refugee camps; or young men's educational failure may result in gang violence, which damages the whole community. Secondly it is still common for gender to be considered a women's issue that can only be addressed by looking at women's needs and interests, without addressing the barriers created by gender relations, men's roles, and the gendered nature of institutions.[4] It may be easier for a man than a woman to understand these masculine attitudes and controls and, in so doing, to identify possible entry points for initiating change. When it is necessary to challenge the barriers, it may again be easier for a man, for if a woman does so, she may be perceived to be confrontational and 'rocking the boat'.

Resistance

A man may be better able than a woman to uncover and understand the 'politically incorrect' but deeply held views that many men (and some women) have about gender. He may therefore have a better grasp of how to deal with instances of personal and institutional resistance to concepts of gender equality, whether within his own organisation or within programmes and projects in partner countries. Overseas, women may have real difficulties in learning the true perceptions of local men. Men may be either disrespectful or alternatively cautious in expressing their true opinions.

In contrast, there are some areas where men are likely to be at a disadvantage, compared with women. Overall, there are more men than women who find working on gender issues uncomfortable – who seemingly seek to avoid the potential conflicts. This has limited the effectiveness of some social-development advisers in giving prominence to gender-equality concerns. Advancing the position of women can pose a challenge to men's identities that they are unwilling to address. It is perhaps worth noting that those men who have taken senior gender positions have for the most part already established themselves successfully in their organisations. (Otherwise, maybe, they would not take the risk!) They are volunteers, committed to taking up the challenge, and are thus a valuable asset.

Advantages and disadvantages of women being responsible for promoting gender equality

Knowledge, commitment, and experience

Women gender specialists may bring considerable prior knowledge to their jobs. Female students are much more likely to have studied gender subjects at university than men. Very few men, particularly British men, choose gender options as undergraduates or go on to

7

do master's degrees in gender or women's studies – indeed, they are effectively excluded from some master's courses. Once within a development organisation, in situations where there is a choice, women staff are more likely to attend gender training, particularly advanced training.

Because gender-equality objectives are overwhelmingly about reducing women's disadvantage and powerlessness, women gender specialists are more likely than men to have a strong personal commitment to their work. Many gains on women's issues have been achieved as a result of their steady, tenacious persistence.[5] However, the passion that such women feel also acts to their disadvantage: it may be perceived by men as illogical and occasionally embarrassing. Women gender specialists have also had to develop skills to make the most of small chances to further gender-equality policies and to devise flexible ways of moving ahead in the face of overt and covert opposition.

Sisterhood networks and communications

Women have the tremendous advantage of 'authenticity' when championing gender equality — although, if they are wise, women gender specialists are fully aware of the complexities, and particularly the limitations of the concept of shared experience. (A man, however, can never have the same insights as a woman into some dimensions of gender, such as those associated with child-bearing.)

Both at the policy and the project levels, a woman is better able than a man to harness sisterhood solidarity. It is easier for a woman gender advocate to build alliances with women allies within official structures such as the European Commission or DFID. She can gain support from women's networks and gender and development networks, for example NGOs, academic groups, and North–South partner-ships. Potentially women are better able than men to make contact with women in developing countries.

In country offices, women can communicate more easily with women partners and women beneficiaries, partly because of assumed common experience, and partly because strong cultural barriers may restrict men's ability to talk with women. Several men commented to me that at the project level, a man has much less access to both women leaders and women beneficiaries. This restricts understanding and

especially the quality of the feed-back that is so essential to ensure effective implementation.

Practicalities

In the field, it may be easier for expatriate women or upper-class women partners to take on a male role — to join men's gatherings as honorary men for professional purposes — than it is for a man to adopt a woman's role and sit in women's gatherings. The honorary male role is certainly well recognised in many countries. (The converse may also be possible. I have seen male social organisers informally discussing family planning with women's groups in northern Pakistan, seemingly assuming a temporary role as honorary females.)

Women, however, face practical problems in their work in a way that men do not. Women staff are often less physically mobile, particularly at the important mid-management level, for personal and family reasons. Overseas offices need a good mix of men and women staff, if their gender-equality policies are to seem credible to partners. DFID are presently examining why so few women staff are taking up posts abroad. More family-friendly personnel policies may be the answer. Once overseas, women may face difficulties in travelling unaccompanied: they may be harassed, or their behaviour may simply be considered inappropriate.

Reflections

All the men and women gender specialists whom I contacted in my research are convinced that men have an active part to play in implementing gender-equality policies, although this usually means advancing the position of women. Nevertheless, doubts and questions remain. Some relate to personal matters and some to the political sphere.

- For example, will men still promote equality in situations where there is not a win–win solution, but when they personally or collectively have to give up power or personal comfort? This may not be a major consider-ation for men in donor organisations, but it is certainly a risk where local men are championing gender issues in partner countries.
- How easy is it for women activists, whether inside a donor organisation or on the outside,

to set aside the collective memory of discrimination and provide men gender specialists with the support they will need? Experience so far has been limited, but generally women gender experts have welcomed men. In some instances there has been initial hesitation, but this seems mainly to have been hidden from the man concerned. Only occasionally have women's NGOs or women consultants been outwardly critical.

- Are men who lead on gender simply perpetuating male dominance by 'speaking for women'? Using men as gender specialists could lead to men regaining power even in the field of gender, where women have exercised autonomy and authority. Moreover, will the result of including men be to delay the more transformational changes needed in the organisation? Men in a bureaucracy tend to be conservative – less willing to challenge the status quo than women. Moreover, a man promoting gender can give the impression that it is only a professional matter: the deeply embedded personal and political aspects, which need to be addressed if permanent change is to be achieved, may escape the attention that they should be given.

There are also more general concerns over outreach.

- How can donors and partners check the 'evaporation' of gender policies which so often occurs during implementation?[6] The causes are many, but the attitudes of powerful male stakeholders and institutional barriers which effectively exclude women are critical.
- Have bilateral donor agencies the necessary sensitivity to local conditions and the willingness to adapt their own agendas to respond to the views and perceptions of local partners, and to recognise that local priorities for the advancement of women may be valid, though different from their own? The allegations about the imposition of white, Western feminism on developing countries have largely subsided, but they have left an unfortunate legacy. One way of dealing with the accusation that donors are 'interfering' in other cultures is to support local agendas to promote gender equality.
- More prosaically, will gender staff — and staff are desperately overstretched in many donors' field offices — have the energy to

respond to unexpected opportunities which may arise because of the quickly changing dynamics of gender relations in partner countries?

Challenges for the way ahead

There are major challenges if gender equality is to be effectively and holistically addressed in development practices over the next few years.

As the DAC Review showed, top managers (*de facto* senior men) need to demonstrate greater commitment and give better leadership to their staff, particularly male staff. Such commitment needs to be reflected in more resources, both financial and human. Almost three-quarters of gender units surveyed in the DAC Review have only between one and five members of staff.

The status of gender activities needs to be raised by demonstrating and celebrating success, providing incentives, and requiring staff accountability. Raising the profile of gender activities is, of itself, likely to attract more men, as well as women, to promote gender policies. Implementers need more support, in terms of expertise (guidelines and specific technical tools). Regular monitoring from a gender perspective can provide learning opportunities, as well as keeping intentions on track. Gender specialists need to focus on new areas of emphasis such as human rights, conflict resolution, programme aid, and poverty reduction, in order to ensure that they can contribute effectively 'ahead of the game'.

Above all, I would suggest, gender units (or their social-development equivalents) need mixed teams for greater credibility and for greater versatility. As this paper has shown, men and women gender specialists have complementary understanding, skills, and approaches. They have overlapping constituencies, relating most effectively to different groups of stakeholders. As DFID has shown, there are great advantages, along with some risks, in having both men and women professionally responsible for gender.

To conclude, taking or reinforcing these steps will provide the opportunity for bi-lateral donors to make a real improvement in the provision of effective, gender-sensitive support to overseas partners in their development efforts.

Notes

1 I particularly want to thank Phil Evans, my successor in DFID. Our joint discussions inform this paper. I am also very grateful to Hazel Reeves, director of Bridge, for enormously constructive comments on the draft.

2 The DAC Statement is available in hard copy and on the web as 'Gender Equality: Moving Towards Sustainable, People-Centred Development', OECD/DAC Paris, 1995. The short version of the Review is similarly available as 'Progress towards Gender Equality in the Perspective of Beijing + 5: Beijing and the DAC Statement on Gender Equality', OECD/DAC Paris 2000. The Review was carried out by Bridge, IDS Sussex; I assisted in a supporting role.

3 See also another presentation from this seminar series, published as Farnsveden and Ronquist 2000.

4 There have been unfortunate examples of projects designed to empower women which led to backlash and violence, because the views of the men in the community had not been taken into account.

5 Sometimes women have been unwilling to compromise 'as good chaps should'!

6 See, for example, Longwe 1997.

Bibliography

DAC (1995) 'Gender Equality: Moving Towards Sustainable, People-Centred Development', Paris: OECD/DAC

DAC (1996) 'Shaping the 21st Century: The Contribution of Development Co-operation', Paris: OECD/DAC

DAC (2000) 'Progress towards Gender Equality in the Perspective of Beijing + 5: Beijing and the DAC Statement on Gender Equality', Paris: OECD/DAC.

Farnsveden, U. and A. Ronquist (2000) 'Why men? A pilot study of existing attitudes among SIDA's staff towards male participation in the promotion of gender equality and development', *IDS Bulletin* 31: 79-86

Longwe, S. (1997) 'The evaporation of gender policies: a feminist perspective', *Gender and Development* 5: 10-16

Woroniuk, B., H. Thomas, and J. Schalwyk (1996) 'Mainstreaming Gender' and 'Gender Equality Action Plans: a Think Piece', SIDA

Middle-aged man seeks gender team

Chris Roche

If you don't want to read about the experience of a white middle-class, middle-aged, married man with two children, working on gender issues, skip this contribution. If you do, at least now you know where I am coming from! I have worked with colleagues engaging with gender issues for the past ten years, and during that time I have questioned and developed my understanding of and conviction about working on gender relations, and about those who promote gender equity.

Probably the most important events that changed my attitudes to gender were living with a polygamous family in a West African village for one year, and becoming a father. Until recently, I have never really deliberately interpreted and built upon these experiences, but now I am recalling them and analysing what shaped my idea of gender roles and relations. As a parent who would like to spend more time with his children, am I at a point of my life when it is in my interest to challenge traditional notions of what it is to be a man? If we can assume that at least some non-poor people are willing to make sacrifices in order to achieve economic and social justice for the poor (such as changing their life-style or paying higher taxes), why should we not assume that some men are willing to let go their privileged position in favour of gender equity? If I am willing to do so, what challenges lie ahead, both for me and for Oxfam GB – the organisation in which I work?

Gender issues and organisations

The relationship between the individual and the organisation is critical. Oxfam GB, like any organisation, is composed of staff with their own identities, interests, and opinions. Various aspects of these will dominate in various settings; gender is one of them, but there are also class, race, age, disability, and other dimensions of difference. However, many would argue that, at least at the apex of power, the dominant identity of most Northern NGOs such as Oxfam is white, middle-class, and 'male'.

This is not, of course, the only imbalance in organisational identity. White, middle-class, 'female' interests might predominate over, say, black, working-class, 'male' interests.

The first lesson that a man working on gender issues learns is that what he has to say is sometimes discounted. My first brush with such 'identity politics' was particularly upsetting because, in other places, my views have hitherto been listened to as a matter of course — even if it was because I was a man. It takes some time to learn what it is like to be excluded or ignored. It takes even longer before you wonder whether what you had to say before had any inherent value, or whether your gender simply made your views seem more coherent and more readily accepted, especially in an organisation that shares your identity.

Next I learned that trying to discuss with colleagues the importance of incorporating a social analysis into their work quickly induces a sort of 'gender deafness' and 'glazed-eye syndrome'. So whatever prior advantages I had as a man, for some people the subject matter of my work seems to have made me less interesting, perhaps less coherent, and almost certainly more tedious. Those glazed eyes are not only male, which indicates the complex relationship between personal identity and the organisation, often perceived as male-dominated, or having a male identity.

Men's influence on men should not be underestimated. As we see in public-policy advocacy, 'insider' strategies, i.e. using discreet private lobbying rather than public campaigning, are an important part of changing the attitudes and behaviour of others. Men have not yet been trained and used as gender-equity advocates at Oxfam as women have, but this should be part of any transformation strategy. However, men who wish to undertake this role must accept that, in the eyes of some, they can never win. If they succeed as gender-equity advocates, this will simply confirm that the institution listens to men rather than women. If they fail, critics will say that they lack true commitment or conviction. Once again, this is a hard, but

11

rewarding, lesson to learn for men who are used to being personally associated with success. It is also a good test of whether one is more concerned with getting good ideas adopted than with personal recognition!

Debate and dialogue

If we do want more men, and women, to act as advocates for gender equality, 'gender experts' must be more prepared to engage in debate and to be challenged. Sometimes many men, and some women, in the organisation feel that they cannot really question or debate certain issues, because it will be seen as a lack of commitment to 'gender'. Staff in Oxfam mentioned this to me on a number of occasions before I joined, and it is interesting that they felt more able to confide this to a man, even a man who works on gender. Equating commitment with the extent to which people do or do not understand notions of gender equality can lead to an uncritical, superficial acceptance of the 'right' views, opinions, and rhetoric. This is dangerous, because people who do not fully understand ideas of gender equality are not necessarily resistant to them (although this may well also be the case); it may be that the ideas simply have not been adequately discussed, understood, and argued over. These people may therefore be surprised when they delve into feminist literature and discover that a lot of the questions in their minds that they did not dare to voice — about men's role in society, about the relationship between gender and class or ethnicity, about whether there is one feminism or many, about whether the world would be a better or more equal place if it were run by women — are the subject of intense debate and argument.

There is a growing sense in the North that the world is more complex, diverse, and uncertain than we are often led to believe, and that well-known theories which explain the truth of the universe are in fact fallacies. As a consequence, any theory that claims a monopoly of knowledge or offers a single explanation for complex problems is increasingly viewed with suspicion or disbelief. Unfortunately, much of the discourse on gender has followed this trend, in order, as Ruth Lister puts it, to challenge male 'universalist' views and to unmask the 'female non-citizen' beneath. But this necessary challenge to a 'false universalism' has now itself been questioned by those who no longer simply want to oppose 'male' universalism with 'female'

universalism. These critics reject the single category 'women' and wish to define other dimensions of identity as equally, or more, important in various contexts.

In a development organisation such as Oxfam, a lack of debate and education on matters of gender equity and social diversity can result in people simply using the 'right' language for planning or evaluating programme work, instead of carrying out the necessary analysis of complex social relations and contextual difference. This has been evident in a number of country strategic plans, and the organisation has accepted such superficial usage of its Gender Policy. I fear that correcting the alleged absence of feminist language in Oxfam may simply lead to further acceptance of certain words, but not to a greater insight into how women's status can be improved, and how this aim requires different strategies to be implemented in different places. Moreover, debates must also be grounded in a solid evaluation of case studies, so that the various strategies that are adopted to implement Oxfam's Gender Policy can be compared properly.

Open and honest debate at the organisational level should encourage men to gain more than a superficial commitment to gender issues. With a greater intellectual conviction of why and how gender equality can and should happen, men will not merely be encouraged to change their attitudes towards women and towards themselves (which we increasingly understand as necessary), but will build on this knowledge in their own lives. We can make allies among men who will then behave in a gender-sensitive way when 'unsupervised' and act as advocates for change among their colleagues, family, and friends.

The importance of communicating new ideas

Considering the above, it is perhaps all the more surprising that less effort goes into ensuring that the arguments for gender equity and the insights offered by feminist debate are clearly presented and debated, than goes into gender training (and other aspects of building capacity on gender issues). I am particularly surprised, because those arguments seem to me so compelling, and the insights of some feminist analysis so exciting. This may sound like the typical reaction of a man who feels uneasy about exploring his own attitudes and behaviour, which forms an important part of gender training and other capacity-building initiatives. Personal exploration must be buttressed and complemented by intellectual argument, which will reinforce the desired attitudinal and behavioural change. Of course it is important to open up the organisation to feminist ideas, but I feel that there is sometimes a danger of focusing on the language of feminism, rather than the ideas and debates that it describes.

Clearly there is a relationship between the words of transformation and the ideas of transformation. Failure to achieve change is often blamed not so much on the language, but on people's inability to understand or accept the ideas and concepts represented, particularly in the case of concepts that challenge the *status quo* of power relations. In this analysis, the failure to put new ideas into practice is blamed on those people who do not understand them, rather than on those people who communicate them inadequately. One aspect of adequate communication is to be open to challenge and discussion. In Oxfam, some new or rediscovered concepts, such as social capital and civil society, have been subject to intense questioning, and the proponents of these ideas welcomed debate. However, there has been a lack of open discussion of gender theory. It seems that sometimes intellectual curiosity and challenge are acceptable for some concepts, but not for others.

This raises another question about Oxfam's organisational culture and the distribution of power. To what degree does the organisation encourage or discourage debate on gender issues, compared with other issues? To what extent are such debates limited to a small group of the converted, rather than addressing a wider audience? And to what extent does Oxfam encourage any debate on development, when so much time is spent discussing internal procedures and processes? The changing organisational culture of development NGOs, which some would argue has been one of growing managerialism, leaves little space for thinking about our 'core business'. This imposes severe constraints on potential allies to enter into necessary debates on development, and on gender issues in particular.

Exciting ideas

So what exciting ideas does feminist thinking and analysis offer a man like me, working in an agency such as Oxfam?

Ideas about institutions and organisations

Naila Kabeer's Social Relations Approach[1] and Anne-Marie Goetz's writing on gender and institutions[2] provide particularly rich material for an agency endeavouring to link micro and macro processes of development, and to influence the policies and practices of those institutions that perpetuate poverty and inequality. In addition, their work elucidates how organisations are at the same time both the product of the society in which they are situated and actors in reproducing that society. This helps us to understand how male interests (or any other set of interests) become institutionalised, and how Oxfam must therefore transform itself if it is to maximise its impact on society. Kabeer's work in particular shows the importance of the household, for it is at this level that broad social trends actually affect people's daily lives; more generally, the nature of family or household relations is a critical determinant of how societies function.

These are just two examples of the many authors who have contributed to our under-standing of organisations and institutions, and whose work would be useful to a wider, non-specialist audience.

Ideas about the link between economic and social relations

The traditional divide between economics and social studies has been challenged by Nancy Folbre and Diane Elson, among others. Folbre's wonderful caricature of a debate between a Marxist economist, a neo-classical economist, and a feminist economist — which not only gives the reader a good insight into basic economic theories but also challenges some fundamental premises of both the 'left' and the 'right' — should be compulsory reading for all Oxfam programme managers.[3] Diane Elson's suggestions for how to ensure a sound integration of gender into macro-economic analysis should form part of our strategic-planning guidelines.[4] Both authors challenge the established division between economic production and social reproduction (the way in which societies care for children and other dependants), which has been ignored by conventional economics. Folbre offers intriguing insights into the ways in which both of these are shaped by various interrelated interests, which compete and co-operate at different times. These interests exist and are played out at all levels: from the State to the household, and even at the individual level. I am thus an employee, a consumer, a manager, a father, and a middle-class white man all at the same time; different elements of my identity will predominate in different contexts.

Elson emphasises that there are arguments on the grounds of efficiency as well as equity for promoting women's status and empowerment. (In other words, gender equality is desirable not only for moral reasons, but also because it will enable women to contribute to economic development.) Like Folbre, Elson offers some explanation for why, if it is beneficial to society, gender inequality is still allowed to persist. The first, kinder, interpretation is that men do not understand that short-term losses will lead to long-term gains. The second one concludes that it is in the interests of the powerful — usually men — to pay the price of lower efficiency in order to retain control.[5]

Men and masculinity

Not surprisingly, I find the recent interest in men and masculinity especially absorbing. A recent issue of Oxfam's journal *Gender and Development* (GAD)[6] offers challenging ideas and insights which resonate strongly with my own experience. These include the suggestion that there are aspects of the male role which do not actually suit my personal preferences; that women as well as men may have good reasons to preserve the status quo in gender relations; that 'social fatherhood' (in other words, the part played by fathers in their children's social development) is an important role; that male violence, and the links between violence, the socialisation of boys, and their livelihood options in particular, need greater study. I also welcome Sarah White's challenge to the caricature of the unhelpful man:

'Good girl / bad boy' stereotypes present women as resourceful and caring mothers, with men as relatively autonomous individualists, putting their own desires for drink and cigarettes before the family's needs.[7]

Of course it is quite easy to agree with, and push for, changes that are in my interests and suit my preferences: less time at work equals more time at home with the kids; a better social environment means less worry about my and my family's security; improved government expenditure on health and education services, paid for by progressive taxation, means lower potential expense for me; more women in the army, and there is less chance that they might have to call up unfit 40-year-old men. There is therefore a comprehensive, important agenda for change which would further the interests of both women and men — and this agenda must be elaborated more thoroughly.

It is of course more difficult to accept the cost of realising those aspects of gender equity that challenge my own status or power, where it is not a 'win/win' situation. These range from the relatively simple — would I, and my two male colleagues, be prepared to use the toilet upstairs so that my 17 female colleagues, who now share one toilet downstairs, could convert the 'gents" to a 'ladies"? — to harder, usually more personal, questions about roles and responsibilities at home and at work. I also wonder whether I would be prepared to forgo a promotion in order that the position would be won by a (gender-sensitive or feminist) woman. These situations are less clear-cut, and involve considerable sacrifice of power and privilege.

Putting ideas into practice

Feminist authors provide ideas and perspectives that go to the heart of how societies and organisations function. Their work uncovers how seismic changes in societies, including industrialised societies, can occur without a single macro-economic indicator picking up on them — how we raise and care for children; how and where men's and women's gender interests may complement or compete with each other — and they analyse the complex interaction of economics, politics, and social institutions. However, these ideas and concepts are often cloaked in a form that is impenetrable to busy field workers and managers. They need translation into simpler language, but they also need to be transposed to fit people's own lives and experiences. The challenge is to use these concepts and insights in a way that is relevant to the specific context. The authors who have inspired me cannot answer, on my behalf or that of other men, the more difficult question of how we deal with our own power and privilege; but they can certainly provide food for thought.

Another challenge for development workers is to think more deeply about how the lessons that we learn from the women whom we encounter and work with around the world, whose daily struggles we witness, can be better synthesised and shared, and how they might bring about change. Thus we must bring together and link the insights gained from practice as well as from theory.

There is much to be done in interpreting gender concepts both 'up' (i.e. from practitioners) and 'down' (i.e. from theoreticians). Those working on gender issues in Oxfam must communicate in both directions if they are to add value in the process of sharing and generating knowledge. This is a difficult balancing act. In addition, they must also balance the inflow of others' ideas into the organisation with Oxfam's sharing of its own experiences. It is all too easy either to be sucked into interminable internal processes or to abandon all hope of achieving organisational change and thus to communicate only externally. In our work on gender equality, where the relationship between an organisation and its environment is so critical (as Goetz and others have shown), operating both on the inside and the outside, in a complementary way, is critical.

Can NGOs achieve gender equity?

In summary, being a man working on issues of gender equity demands persistence and the courage to challenge and debate issues until one understands them, to study feminism and engage with feminist debates, and to be prepared to debate and argue with colleagues and friends. It also means working out how one's personal interests are translated into organisational interests, and how one's personal behaviour interacts with organisational culture.

If we accept that most Northern NGOs are white, middle-class, and 'male' in identity, can we really expect these organisations to check their dominant interests in support of those who might undermine them? For an individual such as myself, whose personal identity seems well aligned with the dominant interests, I believe that this is difficult, but not impossible; for an organisation, it must be much harder. Perhaps the first step is to recognise that the organisation's normal practice, its 'default option', is always liable to favour dominant interests, and that the price of transformation is eternal vigilance.

Notes

1   Naila Kabeer (1994) *Reversed Realities*, London: Verso.
2   Anne-Marie Goetz, 'Institutionalising women's interests and gender-sensitive accountability', *Development Bulletin*, Vol. 26, No. 3.
3   Nancy Folbre (1994) *Who Pays for the Kids? Gender and the Structures of Constraints*, London: Routledge.
4   Diane Elson (1995) *Male Bias in the Development Process*, Manchester University Press.
5   Diane Elson (1997) *Gender-aware Country Economic Reports: Concepts and Sources*, Working Paper No. 1, Manchester: Manchester University Press.
6   *Gender and Development*, Vol. 5, No.2, 1997.
7   Ibid.

Men in the kitchen, women in the office? Working on gender issues in Ethiopia

Feleke Tadele

In this short paper, I attempt to assess the opportunities and constraints that exist for men who work on gender issues. In particular, I wish to share my own experience as a man employed by Oxfam GB in Ethiopia. I particularly examine the challenges and the opportunities that I have experienced over the last four years, during which time we have formally engaged in the promotion of gender issues in development projects and the formulation of gender strategies and policies.

Oxfam GB began its field operation in Ethiopia in 1974; the operation was scaled up after the famine of 1984–85. We presently run programmes which address three key issues: food security and livelihoods, civil and human rights, and social-service provision. We aim to promote gender equity across all these three areas of work. In 1997, we started to develop a women's-rights strategy for use during the next period to 2000. The Addis Ababa office has begun the process of training its staff in the tools of gender analysis, and attempts are being made to incorporate gender-related aims in routine objective-setting and work-planning. Beyond Oxfam, there are opportunities to address gender-related issues in Ethiopia, in the policies and programmes of government and non-government organisations.

In comparison with many other African countries, statistics on gender-related issues look bleak in Ethiopia. Despite their equal share with men in socio-economic life, Ethiopian women have little decision-making power and a smaller share of resources and benefits. Eighty-seven per cent of women in Ethiopia are engaged in agriculture, contributing about 50 per cent of income based on subsistence agriculture (UNICEF 1993). However, little attention has been given to involving women in rural development efforts and enabling them to benefit directly from agricultural extension services. Girls make up only 33 per cent of school enrolments, and the drop-out rate is very high. Among educated women who work in the formal labour force, only 11 per cent have management posts, and most are engaged in manual and clerical jobs. The average number of children born to Ethiopian women is currently estimated at 7.7 (CSA 1993), and the rate of contraceptive use is about 4 per cent among women of child-bearing age (CSA 1993). This is a very low rate in comparison with other African countries such as Kenya (23 per cent), Botswana (30 per cent), and Zimbabwe (32 per cent).

Such statistics offer compelling evidence for the need to work on gender-determined power relations and to promote women's rights. Such work has begun, at least in theory, at government level and within the NGO sector. Ethiopia has a national gender policy in place, and desks for women's affairs have been established within various government departments. A number of local and international NGOs have been encouraging debate and the development of subsequent action to address women's needs. However, at present, these policies are still a long way from succeeding in delivering their goals of affirmative action by a strong women's movement, one that is able to address gender issues effectively. In the past, women's organisations have been part of the State political apparatus, and a civil movement has not yet become apparent.

Some people still associate women's issues with the negative experiences under the socialist regime in Ethiopia. The Revolutionary Ethiopia Women's Association was established at a national level during the revolution in the mid-1970s. Despite the association's effort to promote projects which directed resources at women, more attention was given to the political position of women. As socialism rooted its philosophy in the question of class struggle, gender issues were considered only as a factor that contributes to class differentiation. 'Power' was the main question, and radical changes in the position of women were promoted. As a result, there is a popular perception that some women abused their rights within their families, trying to achieve a radical exchange of roles with their husbands. This is believed to have included rejecting the role of child-care,

16

showing disrespect for existing family rules, and spending too much time at political meetings away from home. The current interest in gender relations is thought by some people to be no different from those days. Working on gender issues is therefore difficult, because some think that the same things are being propagated in a different format, as part of the new political agenda in Ethiopia. In relation to this, there is a tendency to assume that the women who work in the gender movement are 'Westernised', with a weak relationship with their culture and religion. This, it is alleged, is proved by their 'lack of commitment' to going and working with rural women. Working with urban middle-class women's groups and organisations is considered fashionable, or Westernised, and irrelevant to the 'needs' of grassroots women.

The comparative rarity of women employed in the workplace in Ethiopia makes it particularly noticeable that one sector — gender issues — is dominated by women. In the Ethiopian context, women's educational opportunities are low, and this practical constraint on women's employment is a major reason why the vast majority of formal-sector posts go to male employees. In 1997, Oxfam itself had 70 staff in Ethiopia; only five were female, and one of these was the expatriate Director. Yet, because people assume that gender is a women's issue, it is assumed that a post concerned with gender should be filled by a woman. The overall scarcity of educated women in paid employment, and the fact that gender is seen as a women's issue, can lead to a ghettoisation of gender concerns.

My own experience works against this trend. I started to work as the contact person on gender issues four years ago, as part of my responsibilities for advising Oxfam's Ethiopia programme on community development and civic/human rights. I was happy to accept the responsibility for gender work, for three reasons. First, as a sociologist, I believe that gender inequalities in Ethiopia are mostly the result of the norms and values with which our society defines the roles and responsibilities of women and men. Action to redress this problem is, therefore, the duty of sociologists like myself; and this action is the responsibility of both women and men. Second, in my view little attention has been given to the task of involving Ethiopian women in development initiatives, and enabling them to benefit from such programmes. Thus, I feel that my action on gender issues could contribute to increase the involvement of women. Third, NGOs like Oxfam GB and its partners, given their resources and commitments, are among the main agents working for the promotion of women's rights. Hence, my post within Oxfam means that I am in the right position to act.

Opportunities and disadvantages for men who work on gender

One advantage for me as a man working as a lead person on gender is that my job gives me dual positions in debates on gender. I speak both as a man — a gendered person — and as a 'gender specialist'. Provided that men recognise that gender issues affect the ways in which power relations between women and men are played out, it should be obvious that they are as close to the issues as women are. I am in a good position to influence the attitudes of other men. Pragmatically, my identity as a man can be used to further the agenda of women's rights, as I am likely to be listened to by both women and men.

Another pragmatic advantage of being a man working on gender issues in Ethiopia is that, at the current time, men do not face the same problems as women face in jobs where they are required to travel extensively in remote areas, sometimes alone. I wish to emphasise that this does not mean that women staff do not travel; but that, due to a mixture of cultural and practical factors, there are constraints on women's mobility at work. First, most educated Ethiopian women are still chiefly responsible for domestic affairs, so women are expected to fulfil their responsibilities at home. As a result, women find it difficult to travel for extensive periods away from home. Many find themselves limiting their work to that which can be done around their home areas. Second, even if a woman is well educated, when she travels out alone she has a greater chance of being harassed than men. We know that these issues are two of the reasons that explain why women are less likely to apply for posts in rural projects than in urban ones; and, as the statistics indicate, Ethiopia is a country where rural development initiatives are a very significant part of NGO work. The majority of women who do apply for employment on rural projects are either single, divorced, or widowed; the married women who apply tend to live in the specific project area.

However, pragmatism apart, men also face significant disadvantages when working on gender issues. The main challenges that I have encountered are outlined below.

The first challenge comes from the fact that women and men experience gender relations so differently. As already noted, gender issues are misunderstood and assumed to be the same as women's issues, and working on gender is therefore assumed to be a woman's job. Thus, many women take it as a joke when they see me in meetings and discussion forums. Even if a man is sympathetic to the cause of gender equity, and has knowledge of the practical and theoretical issues, he may encounter prejudice from those who feel that, since women lose most through gender-determined disadvantage, only women can sense the real issues and can plan necessary changes properly. Some may perceive men who are interested in gender issues as simply joining the gender specialists because gender is a fashion, and it is advantageous to be part of a new movement. These people see development organisations involved in gender issues as simply taking advantage of funds offered for gender-related activities, and individuals working on gender as following a lucrative career path. For some, this is certainly true. Some 'women's' and 'women-oriented' organisations use the current concern for women's rights and gender issues to their own advantage to gain funding, by using the rhetoric only. In my work I often find local NGOs which note gender issues a key concern; some even derive the name of their organisation from gender and development terminology, calling themselves names such as 'Organisation for Women and Development', 'Aid to Women', 'Forum for Women', and the like. As a representative of a Northern funding agency, one faces challenges when one starts to consider partnership with such organisations. In these organisations, the number of women engaged on the board or in senior management positions is very small; sometimes almost non-existent. When one attempts to analyse the organisation from a gender perspective, ask about more action on gender equality in planned projects, or suggest that more women should be recruited to the organisation, those at the top of the organisation often take it as a real threat to their power. In this way, one discovers that they are not committed or serious about the issues.

Another challenge comes at a personal level. Some people, particularly men, question one's own gender identity. They think that if a man works on gender issues, he must lack a strongly 'masculine' identity. Ironically, the other side of the coin is that if a woman performs the same role, some men will question her gender identity. Because of her pioneering position, she may be seen as a protester, a revolutionary, or a woman who has excluded herself from her culture. It is inevitable that gender work has a significant personal dimension, and we cannot reverse entrenched attitudes on the roles of men and women overnight. Our work can only hope to create an enabling environment, where some perceptions are changed, and the ground paved for more work tomorrow.

For instance, in the case of baking *injera* (Ethiopian bread), this is a duty that is assigned entirely to women. However sensitive I am to gender issues, and however committed my wife is to achieving gender equality, in our cultural context I feel I am prevented from doing the baking. Instead, I sit with my wife and hand her the necessary materials for baking. This might sound amusing or irritating to people who do not know our cultural background, but this is in itself a big shift of role, as compared with my father, who has never been in the kitchen. I am sure that in future our son will share responsibility with his wife more fairly, having been socialised differently by his parents (and of course improved technologies will make the baking business simpler for everyone). Here we can see that there are practical as well as cultural constraints which mean that men find it hard to work on gender issues at a personal level, and that linking one's personal experience into one's professional work becomes difficult.

Finally, there is an issue about ideas of power-sharing. Just as some men consider gender to be a 'women's issue', some 'gender-aware' women consider gender movements only from the viewpoint of women reversing traditional roles or gaining power over men. In my experience, most gender-sensitive men, including myself, feel that gender work should bring equity between women and men. It should not be a process that ultimately creates different sets of power-losers and power-gainers. Men will find it difficult to work on gender issues if women assume that men should be working for their own immediate loss of power, as women gain in power. Instead, both women and men need to be persuaded that gender equity would mean the equal participation of men and women in decision-making.

Conclusion

In the foregoing sections, I have attempted to assess the opportunities and constraints that exist in working on gender issues as a man. I have stated that, while there are relatively few women in employment in Ethiopia, the posts that they do take are often the gender-specialist posts. Only a few men deal with gender issues as their prime responsibility in Ethiopia. There are some good reasons for employing men, from a pragmatic perspective. However, only a few women consider that gender issues could equally well be addressed by men and women specialists. Some women whom I have encountered also allege that if a man works on gender issues he may intensify male power over women, in the sense that women will be perceived as having to speak and act through a male advocate, unable to defend or extend their rights by their own efforts.

However, as other articles in this book argue, gender is about power relations, not exclusively about women's status and needs. Experience teaches that if women alone work for greater equality in gender relations, they face difficulties. If positive changes are to be achieved in gender relations, women, especially the prime movers in the movement, should be convinced that men can play a positive role. As development workers, we can conclude that if we are working towards gender equality and development, we have to exert a greater effort to win the trust and better involvement of men.

References

Central Statistical Authority (CSA) (1993) 'The 1990 National Family and Fertility Survey', Addis Ababa.

UNICEF (1993) 'Annual Report: Ethiopia', Addis Ababa: UNICEF.

Gender training with men: experiences and reflections from South Asia

Kamla Bhasin

I have been organising and conducting informal discussions on women's issues with working-class rural and urban women and with women workers of NGOs almost since the beginning of my development work, which was in 1972. These were participatory and exploratory discussions, in which each us was not only looking for answers but struggling even to formulate the right questions. It was only five or six years after I first became a development worker/activist that I found I was gradually (also) becoming a feminist; which at that time meant recognising that women were the poorest members of the oppressed and exploited castes and classes; were more oppressed and exploited than men; lagged behind their men on almost every measure of health, education, social and cultural status; and experienced myriad forms of violence. The realities of rural India taught me my first lessons about gender and set me off on the long and arduous road towards understanding feminism and becoming a feminist. I realised much later that this journey has no end and no predetermined path. Each of us has to find her own path, stops, and destination.

Because many of us feminist development activists came to feminism via political, trade union, or development activities, we did not believe that all women were oppressed and all men oppressors. Our feminist politics was always connected to our class and/or caste politics. This meant that some (few) sensitive, fair-minded men were always our comrades or partners, even though they were not fully sensitised on matters of gender equity.

In 1983 I organised the first systematic and extended (seven-week) all-women workshop for women development activists from Bangladesh, India, Nepal, Pakistan, and Sri Lanka. This was long before gender and development or 'gender-sensitisation' workshops became fashionable in South Asia. In fact this was even before the word 'gender' gained its present currency. In addition to visiting innovative development/empowerment programmes for women in Bangladesh, Nepal, and India, and

collectively evaluating and reflecting on them, we had a four-day session on concepts and theories related to women and development, conducted by Kumari Jayawardena and Bina Agarwal, both feminist scholars and activists. The response from activists to the conceptualisation sessions was, to my surprise, overwhelmingly positive. That experience led to my organising and conducting a series of workshops, both short and long (four days to four weeks) on gender issues at the local, national, and South Asian levels.

By now, several hundred women have participated in these very intensive, integrated, residential workshops, during which we grapple with a large number of issues related to women and development. We begin these events with the personal experiences of the participants, and we try to understand the patriarchal nature of our societies, as well as the reasons for and the origin of patriarchy or the hierarchical sexual division of labour. We try to break down the barriers between the personal and the political, the personal and the professional, the rational and the emotional, the objective and the subjective, work and joy, and we break down barriers between trainers and trainees, experts and non-experts. Physical exercises, yoga, films, songs, and role-plays are interwoven into these workshops, which are creative, energising, and full of new information and insights. Because, as a facilitator, I do not follow any fixed model and each time start from the experiences, needs, and desires of the participants, every workshop is novel and full of learning and excitement – for me as well as for them.

Since the very beginning, in these workshops we have tried to understand patriarchy in all its different forms and manifestations, and the patriarchal nature of all societal institutions, including family, religion, education, economic organisations and markets, political institutions, legal and State institutions, and the media. In analysing patriarchy, we considered gender relations without using the term 'gender'. Both men and women were under scrutiny in these workshops. It was always stated that it is

20

important to analyse patriarchy as a social system and to understand that men and women have 'feminine' and 'masculine' identities imposed on them through social indoctrination. To understand women, we have to understand men – and *vice versa*. Since women were subordinated by patriarchal structures and they were suffering much more than men, our main focus was on creating a large number of women activists who would lead and/or initiate activities to challenge patriarchy. It was only after several years that we started running separate or mixed workshops with men, to help them to understand patriarchy, men, and masculinities and to devise ways of moving towards gender equality.

The need to sensitise men to gender issues

It was around 1990 that there began to be a demand for workshops on gender issues to be conducted for and/or with men. The demand came from various quarters and for various reasons, as follows.

Women members of rural groups said they were now quite aware of gender issues, and it was time that their men were given a proper 'brain-wash' (*dimaag dhulai*). One of them told us, 'You should now put your cassettes into our men's recorders.' Women activists/development workers found the tensions increasing between men and women workers within NGOs, trade unions, and people's organisations. These women were increasingly dissatisfied with and articulate about subtle and open discrimination against women within these organisations, and they felt that reform should begin at home. They felt that NGO men needed to engage in a critical examination of their own attitudes and behaviour.

Such dissatisfaction was felt also in donor organisations and Northern NGOs, where the women staff were refusing to accept discrimination and double standards within their organisations. They felt it was time that their male colleagues, especially their male managers (managers are almost invariably male, even in the development world!) were trained/sensitised.

In response to the increasing awareness of women's issues, brought about by the global women's movement, several progressive donors started suggesting or insisting on gender-sensitisation workshops for male leaders of the NGOs that they supported.

After doing considerable work with women, some of us women who were involved with training and keen to challenge patriarchy within development organisations recognised now the urgent need to engage in a dialogue with senior male staff of a range of development organisations. Clarity and informed commitment at that level, we felt, were absolutely necessary for promoting women's empowerment and a women's perspective on development. Although everyone could make some 'correct' statements on women's development, most NGO leaders had not yet seriously analysed patriarchy in society and within their own organisations, nor critically examined their own behaviour, attitudes, and assumptions regarding women. Women's issues had indeed been discussed, but as a topic removed from their own experience, which was 'out there' and 'someone else's problem'. Very few men had sat together as a group for any length of time, to look at women's subordination as a system, to understand when and how this system came into existence, to look dispassionately at themselves, their own beliefs, attitudes, and propensity to mis/use power; and to think about their own families, their own organisations, religions, and customs, most of which perpetuate patriarchy and women's subordination. Very few NGO men had seriously reflected on how, as decision-makers and people in authority, they treated their women colleagues and viewed their personal and work concerns. In fact, around this time several cases of sexual harassment of women within NGOs had also come to light, which gave another push to the demands for debate about men, masculinities, and gender relations.

Not only was there a need and a demand for training for men: some of us were also ready to take on the challenge of initiating serious dialogues with them on gender issues. We felt confident, both as facilitators/trainers and as feminists, of handling this task. By 'we' I mean myself, Nighat Said Khan (Pakistan), Vasantha Kannabiran and Abha Bhaiya (India), Khushi Kabir (Bangladesh), Indira Shrestha, Meena Acharya (Nepal), and Sunila Abeyasekera (Sri Lanka), who have been my partners/ co-facilitators in workshops with men. As development activists, we now had enough experience of work at various levels; as trainers we were well equipped and confident; and as feminists we were less angry, more patient, and

21

less confrontational. For all these reasons we felt ready to manage a useful and sustained dialogue with men on sensitive issues. By now some of us had enough grey hair, together with wrinkles and spectacles, to make us look old enough to be 'accepted' as trainers by male decision-makers. (Yet again, we realised that women have to be twice as good as men to be considered as equals.)

Men can and must change

My willingness to engage in a dialogue with men was based on my belief that men can and must change their thinking, attitudes, and behaviour *vis-à-vis* women, especially if they wish to live in a more just and equitable society. I also believe that it is necessary for women to challenge or persuade those men who are our partners/comrades in various struggles and movements to reflect on gender issues, because without a common understanding and shared commitment to change unjust gender relations, it is difficult to be partners with men (or with women for that matter) at home, in organisations, and in social and political movements. I assume that if I, as a middle-class person, can work with and in the interests of the working classes, men can work with and in the interests of women (and in their own long-term interest) in the hope of creating a society without gender hierarchy. As in all other training sessions, in these workshops I begin by affirming the participants, trusting them and believing in their capacity to change, however painful the process of this change may be.

Workshops with men in South Asia

During the last ten years I have conducted more than thirty men-only workshops and about the same number of mixed-sex workshops. The male participants in these workshops are men in decision-making positions in NGOs, governments (in the Maldives), and UN agencies. The NGOs represented vary in size and outreach. Some of them are small, working in a few villages with a team of 10 to 20, while others are very large, with a staff of more than 2000 and outreach to millions of people in thousands of villages (for example, Proshika and BRAC in Bangladesh, and UMN in Nepal).

Several (not all) workshops in Pakistan, India, and Bangladesh were conducted jointly with Nighat Said Khan, Vasantha Kannabiran, Abha Bhaiya and Khushi Kabir and Fawzia Khondkar respectively; in Nepal I conducted them alone, with some sessions facilitated by Meena Acharya and Indira Shreshta. In Sri Lanka, Sunila Abeyasekera joined me, but in the Maldives I conducted them alone. These workshops had 25 to 45 (men) participants, they lasted from three to five days, they were all residential, and normally held in quiet places with simple facilities (NGO training centres, small lodges, or a large room in a village) away from the distractions of cities.

In several of these workshops some heads of NGOs who had confirmed their intention to participate failed at the last minute to turn up, without giving any valid reasons for their absence. Some of us could not help feeling that this low turnout of senior managers was due to the low priority given to gender issues. They probably felt that a session or two, squeezed into a larger conference, was enough to deal with gender: there is no need for a whole workshop on such an issue. Another reason for the low turnout may be the fact that women's issues are considered so commonplace that everyone considers himself an expert on them. Serious classes and study groups, which are deemed necessary for understanding issues of class, caste, community organisation, environment, and even account-keeping and office management, are not considered necessary where gender is concerned. '*What is there to learn on women's issues?*' or '*I have three daughters. Who should know more about women than me?*' seemed to sum up the men's attitude. Such attitudes used to be and often still are a major hindrance to serious reflection on the issue.

Two kinds of gender workshop

Considering the objectives, the underlying ideology, contents, and methodology of the gender workshops/training sessions being offered in South Asia (and perhaps elsewhere too), we find that they are broadly of two kinds:

- those that emphasise project efficiency, which want women to be integrated into the present development paradigm and system;
- those that are transformatory in nature, aiming for radical change in gender relations and the present paradigm of development, which is accused of being ecologically unsustainable and socially unjust.

The purpose of most gender-sensitisation workshops that are organised by official agencies using consultant trainers for male and female policy-makers, planners, and implementers seems to be to enhance the effectiveness of development projects, programmes, and policies; to involve women in development programmes in order to take advantage of their 'productive usefulness', and to ensure that women also benefit from these programmes. Such training mostly uses pre-packaged modules, mainly developed in the North.

The 'official' gender modules do not normally question the mainstream development paradigm which, NGO analysis shows, has further marginalised the poor, and especially poor women, and has worked against the interests of the Third World and the natural environment. These modules prescribe the integration of women within the present system and paradigm of development.

Gender analysis is conducted mainly to understand what exists in the context of the project; but women's lives are larger than projects, and they cannot be reduced to fragments. If women are to be empowered (which is what women and many NGOs now want) and not just 'integrated' into programmes imposed from above, then it becomes imperative to understand and challenge the whole system of patriarchy, and this requires looking deeply at institutions – such as family, religion, culture, law, markets, and the State.

Most gender-and-development packages ignore the whole question of power in gender relations: they depoliticise the issue with the excuse that 'We can't interfere with local culture'. As if these projects do not interfere with just about every other aspect of local life and local culture! What women and NGOs want is gender justice, but this phrase seldom appears in these gender modules.

Moreover, the usual gender modules do not question the patriarchal nature of development organisations, nor do they challenge the experts, policy makers, and implementers to reflect on their own personal attitudes and behaviour. The whole exercise is externalised, dealing with problems 'out there', and making no connections. Threatening local men through gender analysis is fine, but experts, it is argued, should not be threatened, because that will alienate them, rather than win them over for the 'gender cause'. This is another example of fragmented and compartmentalised thinking

which, according to many feminists and many NGOs, should be shunned rather than served up in attractive and well-funded packages.

Most official gender and development workshops fail to talk about or create links between development work and the women's and people's movements for gender equality, environment, peace, democratisation, secularism, and human rights. The usual modules are now being used by some large, well-funded and well-connected NGOs in the South. There is no denying that these modules are useful, in so far as in the context of some projects they make women and their contribution visible, they involve women, and they try to ensure that some benefits reach women. But these modules are inadequate for a large number of NGOs that are seriously questioning the assumptions, rationale, and outcome of many development policies and programmes; that are concerned not only to 'invest' in women but also to empower them, not only to challenge patriarchy at the grassroots level but also to challenge the patriarchal nature of development policies, programmes, and organisations; and that are keen to see the connections between gender hierarchy and hierarchies of class, caste, and race.

Many of us in South Asia have tried to make our workshops transformatory and, in keeping with feminist thinking, integrative and holistic. In these workshops we have tried to do the following:

- To provide conceptual clarity and to help to evolve a common understanding of concepts and issues.
- To create an atmosphere which encourages the participants to reflect critically on their own understanding of gender relations and gender issues, their attitudes and behaviour, and to help them to understand and if possible accept the feminist slogan 'the personal is the political'.
- To become aware of, analyse, and challenge patriarchal attitudes, behaviour patterns, and institutions.
- To develop an understanding of patriarchy, gender, and gender relations in the context of other hierarchies of class, race, and caste.
- To help participants to analyse the nature of development policies and programmes in general, and the policies and programmes of their own organisations in particular, in terms of their impact on women, ecological sustainability, and equity.

23

- To familiarise them with feminist thinking and women's movements, and other people's movements in their own countries and globally.
- To evolve a collective vision of an equitable and gender-just family, community, and society and to develop a strategy to move towards its realisation.
- To create a network of like-minded people and organisations who are committed to gender equality.

Reassuring the (male) participants

Our first task in these workshops is to dispel some of the negative preconceptions that male participants bring along to a workshop of this nature. Since almost all the participants are attending a workshop on gender for the first time, some of them are quite anxious, not quite sure how to respond, behave, or speak. Their insecurities and anxieties stem partly from the fact that, perhaps for the first time in their experience, they are being addressed by facilitators/trainers who are women – and women who are known as strong feminists. During the first few hours of our informal interaction, we hear remarks like: '*So now we are in your hands*'; '*We're ready to be butchered*'; '*We have come to be brain-washed*'; '*So, are you going to convert us?*'; and '*You should really not bother to train men, because it is you women who are your own enemies*'.

In a recent workshop for UN staff, seeing a woman participant eating *gulab jamuns* (brown flour balls in syrup), a male participant joked, '*Oh, now our balls are being consumed*'. The response of many men and women was 'ha, ha, ha', but many others were not sure how to respond. I referred back to the statement on the second day, by which time everyone was at ease.

Such statements are made without any provocation from us, and in spite of our best efforts to avoid being provocative. Often anxiety takes the form of aggression, hostility, and childish stubbornness. But I suppose the very fact of inviting men to a gender workshop is provocative enough, especially for those men who know that a discussion on women's and men's issues will raise uncomfortable questions about matters which are normally not addressed. We find that participants who come from large and hierarchical organisations and are in top and mid-level management positions

are the most insecure, and therefore the most hostile.

Here it should be mentioned that there are many men who are willing to analyse and challenge patriarchy, who are willing to do soul-searching, and who believe that changing the hierarchical nature of current gender relations would benefit everyone.

Clarifying concepts and creating a common vocabulary

After detailed, informal introductions, we ask the participants to write down on a piece of paper their own definition of gender and what they would like to discuss in the workshops. In every workshop we find that no more than one or two people can define gender precisely. We find this amazing, considering the fact that they have all been hearing the word for many years. It seems that no one has bothered to explain to them what the concept means and why it was introduced. Nor have they have ever bothered to ask, or to pick up a book to find out what it is. Typical answers are '*It is men and women both*', '*It is women's issues*', '*male and female sex*', '*equality between men and women*', '*inequality between men and women*'.

There is no understanding of the concept, but there are many misconceived notions: '*It is a Western concept*', '*Women want to be the same as men*', '*It is breaking peaceful families*', '*It is against our culture*'. All these statements are made by very senior NGO managers and government officials, who employ the word 'gender' in all their policy documents.

Another belief articulated by some senior men in two recent workshops was that gender issues are being raised as part of a conspiracy by the 'developed' world against the Third World, and especially against Muslim societies: '*Their own families are collapsing, their women are not getting married or giving divorces, or they are not keen to have children. They want to do the same here.*' Another man, who had followed international debates about human rights, claimed, '*The Western countries are imposing their own ideas on the rest of the world. They now want us to accept and endorse homosexuality in the name of human rights. All this is totally against our beliefs and religion.*' (These men seem to think that gender equality or gay rights have been achieved in the West, or that everyone there believes in them, or that there is no backlash against feminists there !)

In two recent workshops, conducted in May and June 2000, such attitudes were like a wall, and in the first two sessions it seemed that I might not be able to scale or dismantle it. The participants' misconceptions and anxieties had taken the form of aggression, hostility, and total resistance. Finally, the women in the workshops reprimanded their senior colleagues and requested them at least to give me a chance to explain things. However, once all their unfounded doubts and anxieties were dealt with, both these workshops went off very well, and most participants came to me personally to say that they had learned a lot and they had no objection to the way in which I analysed and explained gender. I greeted these admissions with a broad smile and a private sense of satisfaction.

Great gentleness and diplomacy have to be deployed to explain to reluctant participants that they do not understand gender, and then to expound it and related concepts, such as *gender relations, gender division of labour, gendered, gendering, gender bender, gender-blind, gender-sensitive, gender-neutral,* and *gender-transformative.*

Beginning with the personal

As we do with women, in every workshop we try to get men to talk about their personal lives and experiences, their relationships with women at home, at the place of work, and in society at large; to make them see how men benefit from patriarchy; to make them realise that, unlike other issues, gender cannot be dealt with merely as a subject of study, as an intellectual discourse. Changing gender relations, we emphasise, challenges each one of us to reflect critically on ourselves and to make changes, if necessary. Each one of us (men and women) needs to recognise the 'patriarch' sitting inside us, wanting to dominate, and we need to eradicate this tendency. In other words, we challenge the men to recognise, nurture, and value the feminine qualities in them.

Since the session on personal introductions perplexes some participants, we explain the need for them in a programme like this. Getting to know each other well, we explain, is the basis for developing a common understanding and creating solidarity; and in order to know each other well, we have to see each other as a whole; we have to break out of the usual compartments that divide the personal and the official, the

private and the public. We tell the participants that, in our view, challenging patriarchy requires a broad-based movement, and for building that movement we need people who have a common understanding and commitment to gender justice, and who feel close to each other. Because the objective of the workshop is not only to create better professionals, but also to make better, more just human beings, the personal and the public have to be merged.

It is stated many times in the workshops that a person who is sensitive and has empathy for the vulnerabilities of others would also be gender-sensitive, and sensitive to questions of class, caste, and race. Ultimately it is a question of our *insaaniyat* (humanity), our sense of justice and fair play, our human values.

Starting with the personal gives each participant a chance to speak and to realise that everyone has something to share and to contribute. It helps to create an atmosphere of warmth, closeness, and equality. At the same time it gives us trainers an idea of the language skills of participants, each person's level of understanding, and the topics that we will have to discuss and explore. All this makes it easier to plan the contents of the workshop and the level at which the discussions should be pitched to suit every participant.

Sharing our lives and our experiences also helps to root our discussions within our local realities, and to make sense of these realities. Thus, none of our discussions becomes an academic imposition, or a purely intellectual exercise.

Clearing the ground

Knowing well that feminists are easily misunderstood, we make a point of beginning by explaining that we do not look at gender issues in isolation: we see them in the context of larger economic, political, social, and cultural systems, and we believe that changes in gender relations would require changes in other social systems and *vice versa*. In this context, we inform them that our own past and present experiences have not been confined to gender issues, but that we have also engaged with issues related to poverty, caste, class, environment, and human rights.

We also make it clear that we do not have ready-made answers for everything, nor do we believe in promoting the 'correct' line.

We ourselves are searching for answers, and this search, we believe, should be an on-going, dynamic process. In these workshops we try to initiate an honest and earnest dialogue and search for answers, if possible creating a shared commitment to challenging patriarchy and other hierarchies.

We also clarify the fact that we regard women's subordination as a system, and therefore for us it is not a question of men versus women. We know that women too can be patriarchal, and hence we see the need to challenge women's views and attitudes also. Men's views, attitudes, and behaviour patterns are largely created by their up-bringing, so we need to understand the overall system of socialisation and not just blame individual men or women.

In addition to these reassuring or placatory explanations (intended not to 'mother' men, but to facilitate a dialogue), we try to create a relaxed atmosphere by inviting everyone to sing during breaks, by showing films related to our discussions, and generally by making the workshop very informal, participatory, and non-hierarchical (which is exactly what we do in the workshops with women).

The issues

Although the final list and sequence of issues discussed at these workshops emerge only once the event is under way, based on all the questions and doubts expressed by the participants, the issues tend to be more or less the same in every workshop, as follows:

- The situation and position of women and men in the society in which we live and work.
- The concepts of gender, gender relations, gender division of labour, gender formation, etc.
- Patriarchy as a structure and as an ideology, and the origin of patriarchy.
- The patriarchal nature of social institutions like marriage, family, religion, law, media, economic and political institutions, the State, and NGOs.
- Analysis of mainstream development policies and programmes in terms of their impact on ecology, on the poor (especially on women), and on the Third World.
- Analysis of NGO structures, policies, and programmes from the perspective of women, and future strategies and programmes.

- Frameworks and tools for gender analysis and gender planning, and concepts related to them.
- Feminisms and women's movements in the country and globally.
- A vision of families, organisations, and societies without hierarchies of gender and other divisive features.
- Strategies for sustainable and gender-just development.

On every issue, our attempt is to move from social realities to generalisations and concepts. In order to get everyone to speak, we encourage small-group discussions to thrash out most of the issues listed above. As resource people, our task is to fill in the gaps in the discussions, add our views as and when necessary, and provide conceptual/theoretical inputs. On issues with which the participants may not be familiar, or on which they may have what we perceive as wrong notions, we do not hesitate to give lectures. Such issues usually include patriarchy, feminism, gender, the women's movement, and feminist analysis of development. (The contents of these sessions are fairly well covered in several booklets written by me: *What is a Girl, What is a Boy?*, *What is Patriarchy?*, and *Understanding Gender*; and *Some Questions on Feminism* by Nighat Said Khan and me. This is why this present paper is basically concerned with the process rather than the content of the workshops.)

Although the participants are not familiar with the concepts, most of them have a good understanding of the realities of gender. Most participants are aware of (and some are quite articulate on) issues such as women's double burden of work; the active participation of working-class women in production activities, and their contribution to household incomes; men's lack of participation in child-rearing and household activities; the widespread prevalence of discrimination against girls and women in matters of food in-take, health care, education, etc.; the exclusion of women from participating in major decisions within the family and in all decisions in the community; and violence against women.

When invited to do so, the participants are able to generate enough empirical data regarding the subordination of women within and outside the household. It is also fairly easy for them to see how official development programmes and most NGO programmes have been planned and executed by men and oriented to meet men's needs. In fact, the participants themselves provide most of the examples to prove these points.

Some sensitive issues

Problems arise, however, when we try to draw conclusions on the basis of all the information and facts that the participants provide. This is when we sense a certain uneasiness, resistance, and even hostility. To give an example: to explain the position of men and women in the most intimate and crucial social unit, the family, we ask the participants to write on the board examples of the oppression that women and men may suffer within the family. The women's column gets filled in a few minutes. Each participant can give one example or another: female foeticide, female infanticide, sexual assault, psychological harassment, control over women's work and income, discrimination in the provision of health care and education, and so on.

When it comes to listing the oppression or discrimination that men face within the family, the participants have to think really hard to come up with something. All they can think of (and often only with our prodding) are things like 'Men are not allowed to cry', 'Men also have to submit to stereotypes', 'They have to look after women', and 'They have to earn'. However, many participants get extremely upset when, drawing on their data, we conclude that we have to look at power relationships within the family; or when we say that the family can be the location of much injustice and discrimination against women. Suddenly we find some men accusing us of 'wanting to break peaceful families' or 'attacking local culture'. They start expressing fears about the disintegration or the collapse of the family, which would of course mean loss of authority, comforts, and power for men.

At such times we encourage the participants to look at their own reactions and to reflect on them. We argue that thinking critically about the realities of the family and removing the prevalent inequalities and injustice will actually strengthen the family, rather than weaken it. We encourage them to look at the family from the point of view of women, who are at the receiving-end of discrimination. We also provide a historical view of the family, to show how the institution has been changing in response to the changes in the mode and relations of production, and how within the family gender relations have themselves been changing. We try to argue that it is not by feminists that the institution of the family is being weakened, but by all the inequality, injustice, and power struggles that prevail within it. The best way to preserve and make the family a happy place for all, we suggest, is to scrutinise it and change it wherever change is required. We also try to make them understand how power operates within the family.

'You mean patriarchy is a conspiracy by men against women?'

Similarly, some male participants find it difficult to cope with the concept of patriarchy. They are quite prepared to describe all the atrocities against women, but they resist considering them as a system. In fact, some of them actually say 'You can describe women's oppression, but you don't have to look at it as a well thought-out and planned system. We men are not that vicious. Do you mean to say it is a conspiracy by men?'

We find there are some standard responses to criticisms of patriarchy, such as 'We Indians had to subjugate our women when the Muslim invaders came' (as if women in India were free agents before that). The tendency to blame foreigners is not exclusive to politicians! The second very common response is: if there is any problem with women, it is created by other women. Men assert that 'Woman is woman's worst enemy', citing real-life examples of vicious mothers and persecuted daughters-in-law. It is almost comic to observe men who very deftly and passionately analyse caste and class as a system, but are too afraid and resistant (or intellectually dishonest?) to consider patriarchy as a system. Of course, biology is held by many to be responsible for women's subordination.

Another response, normally articulated as an accusatory question, is 'If you are against patriarchy, are you for matriarchy? Is that the solution?' All this is often expressed in highly charged tones, almost as if the women trainers were on trial in the dock. Another accusation hurled at us is: 'You feminists want to be the same as men, and this is against nature.' Some men advise us women 'not to give up your superiority and nobility by trying to copy men'. They are of course quite happy to let men remain 'inferior', 'base', and 'ignoble'.

In a workshop in India, one of the participants quoted some 'great' Indian man (he couldn't name him) who said, 'A woman who wants to be like a man becomes a Raakshasi [a female demon]; a man who tries to be like a woman *becomes a human being.*' The very well-meaning man who quoted this saying never questioned why men are compared to a *Raakshas* (demon). He was only worried about some women becoming demons (like men). We tried to suggest to this friend that it would be more helpful if those men who want to preserve women's 'divinity' and 'superiority' would also challenge men's demon-like nature and encourage them too to be gentle, noble, and superior.

It's the system that needs to be changed, not us

While some participants get worked up when women's subordination is conceptualised as a system, there are others who feel relieved, because they can now blame an abstract phenomenon for everything that is wrong with gender relations. '*You said individual men (or women) have nothing to do with it, it is the system*' is what they claim, to avoid all scrutiny of personal behaviour and attitudes. This of course requires another lecture from us on how all systems are perpetuated by individual actions: women are raped, battered, and insulted not by an abstract system, but by men. All of us together make up the system, and therefore we are responsible for what exists, and we have the responsibility to change the system. So we must oppose not only the unjust system, but also all those men and women who keep it going.

In response to the question whether feminists want to replace patriarchy with matriarchy, we actually feel like picking up our bags and leaving, but, being feminist missionaries (or masochists?), we resist the temptation. Trying (not always successfully) to hide our frustration and anger, we tell them that generally feminists are not so stupid or power-hungry that they would like to replace one unjust system with another. It should be possible, we tell them, to visualise families and societies without hierarchies and inequalities. We also explain that what feminists are asking for is equality, and not sameness. Women do not wish to be like men (especially not like the usual domineering, insensitive men), but they want to have equality and equity. We tell them that if gentleness, caring, nurturing, and selflessness are considered feminine qualities, then we would actually like men to be like women, because the world is in urgent need of these qualities. In several workshops we have had a long discussion of male and female qualities,

after which we conclude that, to be fully human, men and women all need both positive feminine and positive masculine qualities. The present division and separation of these qualities into male and female, we argue, has been good neither for men nor for women. Here is a brief description of this exercise, which we feel clarifies a lot of issues.

An exercise on gendered qualities

After explaining the concept of gender, we remark that spaces, languages, resources, and even qualities may be gendered. The participants are asked to write down on separate pieces of paper what, according to their communities, are male qualities and what are female qualities. These papers are then put on the floor for all to see. This is the kind of list that usually emerges.

Male	Female
Rational	Emotional
Strong	Weak
Smart	Beautiful
Self-centred	Self-sacrificing
Outgoing	Caring
Aggressive	Nurturing
Competitive	Submissive
Brave	Shy
Creative	Calm
Devious	Polite
Fearless	Sensitive
Impulsive	Cunning
Honest	Soft
Tough	Introvert
Violent	Compassionate
Hardworking	Enduring
Opportunistic	Persevering
Insensitive	Quiet
Extrovert	Timid
Dominating	Tolerant
Fearful	Stupid

The next question is: which of these qualities (in both columns) are negative? *Aggressive, self-centred, dominating, devious, violent, insensitive* in the 'male' column and *weak, fearful, shy, stupid* in the 'female' column are declared to be negative qualities without any hesitation. But there is a lot of discussion of whether *ambitious, competitive, go-getting,* and *subservient, obedient, emotional* are negative or positive qualities. Is it a weakness to be emotional, to feel and to show one's feelings? Can anyone be exclusively emotional or exclusively rational? Isn't it a burden for men to be told 'men should not show their feelings' or 'men don't cry'? Being ambitious and competitive is seen as positive by some and as negative by others. At this point some participants usually comment that the negative 'female' qualities, like subservience, shyness, and self-abnegation, harm the women themselves; whereas 'male' negative qualities like aggressiveness, dominating nature, and selfishness are qualities that harm others.

Next in this exercise, we explore the idea that masculine qualities are those that are required for people working in the public sphere, which requires competition, self-centred behaviour, and toughness. 'Female' qualities are those that are necessary for the domestic and community spheres, which need nurturing and caring. So there was once perhaps a logic in inculcating 'male' and 'female' values in societies where the public and domestic spheres were clearly demarcated and assigned to men and women respectively. However, we question if it is now wise or possible to have two separate and opposite set of values for these two spheres. Today, because of women's extensive participation in the public, this logic does not quite hold good any more. It is pointed out that women who work in senior positions in organisations face conflicting demands. Their organisations expect them to be tough and competitive, but their families want them to be subservient and self-sacrificing. It is often very difficult for women to cope with these conflicting expectations and demands.

Next we ask which qualities in the list may be ascribed to which categories if we replace 'male' and 'female' by 'upper class' and 'working class', 'urban' and 'rural', and 'First World' and 'Third World'. It is obvious to most participants that there is a correspondence between 'male' characteristics and conventional notions of what it means to be 'upper class', 'urban', and 'First World'; and a similar correspondence between 'female' qualities and notions of 'working class', 'rural', and 'Third World'. Women, the working class, Third World people, and rural people are supposed to be stupid, emotional, subjective, subservient, etc., as opposed to men, the 'upper class', urban people, and people in the First World, who are supposed to be rational, hard-working, competitive, and ambitious.

Suddenly, it becomes obvious that 'male' and 'female' qualities are the qualities of those with power and those without power; hence, instead of being innate, they are cultivated. The insights gained during these discussions arouse a lively response. Suddenly one of the participants will say excitedly, '*Well, this shows that in a way men treat their women as the urban people treat the rural people, the upper classes treat lower classes, and the First World treats the Third World. There is exploitation and domination in these relationships!*'

Next we ask 'On which side are qualities that are considered superior and prescribed by our religions?' The answer is the 'female' qualities like loving, caring, nurturing, and sensitivity. Buddha, Jesus, Nanak, and Mother Teresa, it is pointed out, aspired to, practised, and prescribed these qualities. So, are women superior to men? Actually, aren't these qualities *human* qualities?

All these questions are not necessarily answered in one session. They are raised in the hope that the participants will start reflecting on them and start finding their own answers. Here the point is made that, although the 'feminine' qualities might be considered superior, current thinking about development promotes the First World, the upper classes, and men as the models that everyone should follow. Isn't everyone encouraged to become ambitious and competitive; and doesn't competition require being self-centred, even dominating others? Does this mean that current development practice is leading the world away from superior qualities? Is this why there is so much disparity in the world, so much wasteful over-consumption in the midst of extreme poverty and misery, so much plunder of the environment, so much war and conflict, so much destruction of community life, even family life? Is this why development has become, in the words of a recent UNDP *Human Development Report*, 'jobless, rootless, ruthless, and futureless'?

The next question raised is: in the interests of sustainable development and regeneration of natural resources, in which qualities do we need more practice, the 'male' or the 'female'? The answer is, of course, the 'female' qualities. Then does it mean that, in the name of development and progress, if more people take on the 'male' qualities, the world will become a more difficult place to live in? Should men become gentler, caring, and nurturing, or should women become more aggressive and competitive?

Finally we pose the following set of questions:

- Is it correct to call these qualities male or female? Are they not all human qualities, and could not anyone decide to practise one or the other?
- Doesn't a good human being need the positive qualities found in the two lists? Wasn't Mother Teresa both strong and gentle, rational and emotional, confident and yet caring, nurturing, and sensitive?
- Aren't human beings incomplete, even a little sub-human, if they have only one set of qualities?
- Doesn't this compartmentalisation lead to oppression and domination and harm men, women, and society?

Here I may go on to ask a deeper (spiritual?) question: shouldn't gender equality mean creating a balance between the positive 'male' and the positive 'female' within each of us? Essentially, gender equality can be achieved only if both men and women give up their lust for power and domination, and also work on their own powerlessness, subservience, and submissiveness. Masculine qualities and macho behaviour patterns come in for a lot of discussion here.

Next we ask if development people are doing enough to preserve and promote human values and principles like love, caring, nurturing, sharing, justice, and equality. Have these values been neglected and marginalised, at the expense of materialistic values? Should we not spend at least as much time, resources, and efforts on fostering positive human values as we do on building strategies and programmes? The best of strategies come to nought if the people implementing them are corrupt and selfish. The unanimous agreement is that we indeed need to focus much more on people, their capabilities and their values. The participants usually accept that the dichotomy between spirituality and development, economics and ethics, science and mortality needs to be questioned and resolved.

This exercise leads to a lot of discussion about NGOs' methods of functioning, their culture and the life-styles of their staff, and their decision-making patterns. It becomes obvious that, if we are serious about sustainable development, we have to review and restructure our organisations, ways of working, and leadership patterns as well as our personal attitudes and behaviour patterns. All these must be based on positive human values. This can be not only

challenging, but also very gratifying. Inner peace and harmony, it is suggested, is much more valuable than outer (material) abundance.

Here I share my belief that men will become more gentle, caring, and nurturing only if they start sharing reproductive work at home, looking after and spending more time with children. The practice of fathering would change men faster than merely discussing these issues in seminars and workshops. We need to start a 'movement of men towards families and family kitchens'. It is only when we spend time nurturing children or nature that we internalise the value of life. If men spend more time in family kitchens and children's playgrounds, they will have less time for engaging in war, be it on the battlefields, on football grounds, on street corners, or within families.

Feminism: much maligned and misunderstood

In most workshops the largest number of questions concern feminism and the women's movement, articulated as follows.

- Isn't feminism imported from the West, and isn't it alien to our culture and religion?
- Isn't feminism an urban phenomenon and therefore quite irrelevant to rural people?
- Isn't feminism confined to 'elite' women who have no idea of the lives and issues of poor, rural women?
- Is feminism woman versus man?
- Don't feminists promote free sex?
- Why is feminism confrontational? Won't it destroy the family, the most important unit in society?
- Why talk of feminism? Why not humanism?
- Why do women want to be like men?

The way in which these questions are formulated and expressed by some participants makes it quite apparent that they are really allegations; they betray discomfort with feminism and feminist formulations and also with some women who call themselves feminists. Although we face such questions all the time, we must confess that we are surprised and quite disappointed when we encounter NGO leaders who claim that they have been working for women's development for years, but who share all the usual misconceptions about feminism and the women's movement. We do expect that at least the senior staff would be a little clearer and better informed, and would have read and thought seriously about these issues.

We normally ignore these loaded questions for the first couple of days, responding to them only after establishing a degree of rapport and covering some ground on women's oppression and women's development. We realise that it would be futile to combat such questions with ready-made answers. Instead we ask participants to list on the board the issues that women's movements or feminists have raised in South Asia, and we then examine them one by one, to see which are Western concerns and therefore not relevant to South Asia, which are urban and not relevant to the rural women, and which are elitist issues and therefore not relevant to poor women.

The board gets filled quite fast with the list of issues that feminists have taken up: dowry, rape, sex-determination tests, female foeticide, equal wages for equal work, income generation, education, property rights, land rights, alcoholism, ecology, unionisation of self-employed women, job reservations, child care, sexism in the media, pornography, women's political rights – the list is unending, and those who had made allegations against feminists also contribute items to it. Even a cursory examination shows that none of them is an exclusively Western concern, and most of them are related to working-class women. Issues like dowry, sex-determination tests, and pornography, which might have been confined to the middle class in former times, are no longer so today.

After dealing with the main misconceptions about feminism and the women's movement, we try to discuss the reasons why they exist, even among sympathetic men. We also speak at length about feminism and the women's movement, their main features, their relevance and significance.

How should religion and tradition be questioned?

In workshops with men, religion and tradition are very sensitive issues, but they cannot really be avoided. While trying to understand patriarchy or gender hierarchy, it is not very difficult to show that — apart from a few biologically linked functions, such as child bearing, breast feeding, and impregnation — there is no activity that is exclusively confined to one sex or the other. But how can one argue

when it comes to questions of faith and belief? Some participants resist any questioning of their religion, or even a historical analysis of religions. What surprises us is that many of these men are dressed in Western clothes, speak English, and indulge in many practices which their religions would not allow.

However, in some workshops it is possible to discuss religions in a historical context and to see that all modern religions were founded by men, that their leadership is almost entirely male (in most, women are by definition excluded), and that the interpretation of dogma and the religious discourses are male-dominated. It is also pointed out that initially many religions (such as Islam, Buddhism, and Sikhism) were revolutionary, in that they challenged existing traditions and established new belief-systems which were more contemporary and more just. Perhaps we should emulate this questioning nature of the founders of our religions, rather than following teaching that was prescribed a long time ago. Because of increasing communalism and conflicts, it is becoming more difficult to have dispassionate discussions on religion and culture, but so far we have managed to discuss this issue very well in some workshops and not so well in others, depending on the degree of openness among the participants.

Masculinity in the twenty-first century

In a few workshops I have been able to share the following thoughts and lead a discussion on them.

- In the twenty-first century, perhaps the biggest threat to human survival is conflict and war. Violence of all kinds (fuelled mainly by economic factors, but also by religious, communal, ethnic, and gender-based differences) is tearing apart the fabric of our nations, communities, and families. Some people are making big money out of wars. Weapons, pornography, and violent films are billion-dollar industries, which enter our homes with the help of TV and the Internet. Young boys are proving their masculinity by fighting in wars, or playing war games, or shooting dead their schoolmates, or having coercive sex with their 'girl friends', or rioting in football stadia. Lust for money and power, ruthless competition, and individualism are rampant. In common parlance, all these are masculine traits, preoccupations, and pursuits. Although women can be and indeed often are violent, greedy, and competitive, if we wish to change the world it is the concept of masculinity that demands to be challenged, and men who have a more urgent need to change.

- But if some men are the problem, there are other men who have offered solutions, including the Buddha, Gandhi, Martin Luther King, Nelson Mandela, and the Dalai Lama.

- Not only masculinity but the whole notion of power needs to be re-examined. Who is more powerful: the one who has power over others, or the one who has power over himself or herself? Hitler or Gandhi? A dictator or Mother Teresa? Is war more powerful than love? If inner power or power over one's emotions of greed, envy, and fear is real power, then men and women both need empowerment. In this sense there may not be any competition between men and women: they will both be working for true human development.

These questions have usually found a resonance in the experience of the workshop participants. One very senior NGO leader, who was earlier strongly opposed to gender workshops, commented, 'If I had known all this is gender, I would never have opposed it.'

Open dialogues help to clarify misunderstanding

Because there is ample time in these workshops (I refuse to lead events that last less than three days), we are able to follow things through and discuss them to a proper conclusion, rather than leaving them mid-way to breed more misunderstandings. For example, participants who make statements like 'All feminists are urban, middle-class women with no understanding of the local culture' are challenged to substantiate their statements by giving examples. In each case we find that the statements have little basis other than a general discomfort with feminism, or a response to some anti-feminist propaganda in the media, of which there is no dearth. In some

cases the anti-feminist sentiments are based on a single encounter with 'an aggressive woman' or 'a woman who smoked'. Our response to such generalisations is to say that judging an extensive movement by the behaviour of one or two women is obviously neither correct nor fair. We do not hesitate to say that, for many of us, becoming a feminist is a long, arduous journey; none of us is perfect, nor do we have well thought-out positions on everything. Very few of us are able to practise everything that we believe in. In this we are no different from socialists or Gandhians or environmentalists.

We find that such dialogues, conducted with as much honesty as we are capable of, do help to reduce hostility, misunderstandings, and misconceptions. By the second or the third day there is much more understanding, warmth, acceptance, and a desire to study and learn more about gender issues. We tell them that in three or four days one can only learn how much more there is to learn, and actual learning will require a lot of reading, discussion, practice, and reflection.

In these workshops, invariably there are men who are gentle, who participate in household work, who bathe their children, who have supported their sisters or wives to get educated, etc. The presence of such men is very helpful in communicating that all men are not the same, just as all women are not the same. This is why the issue is not biological: it is socio-cultural, and — if we want to — we can transform our society and culture.

Once we have dealt with the sensitive issues and basic clarity is achieved, it is fairly easy to discuss and explain issues related to development; how gender-blind planning has been marginalising and disempowering women; and the main tools and frameworks for gender analysis and gender-sensitive planning. We familiarise the participants with all the terms and concepts employed in the discourse of gender relations, such as 'practical gender needs' and 'strategic gender interests'. Basically the attempt is to simplify and demystify ideas: all we need is sensitivity to recognise injustice, and a desire and commitment to challenge it. The tools can be acquired easily.

The written evaluations submitted at the end of every workshop are on the whole overwhelmingly positive. Most participants state that they have learned a lot, they have been forced to think things through, and they have been challenged to reflect on their own beliefs and behaviour. At every workshop the participants recommend that such workshops should be mandatory for all men working in development organisations. Many participants appreciate the connections that are made between gender and other hierarchies of caste, class, and race. This, they say, makes it easier for them to understand gender and gender relations. They also appreciate the fact that all discussions are linked to local realities.

The improved understanding and a desire to move towards better gender relations is also evident when towards the end of the workshop the participants discuss their future strategies for women's development. What they produce is usually clear, comprehensive, and concrete. This is not to say that we succeed in winning over all the men. With one or two, the tensions are never resolved. These men are unable to accept women as trainers and are not open to admitting that they may need to revise/change their attitudes or ideas. However, even these men leave with a lot of questions and a new sense of unease, and that is good enough as a beginning.

Workshops with men are different from workshops with women

We have often asked ourselves how the workshops that we facilitate with men differ from the workshops that we do with women. There are obvious differences. The level of personal sharing is much greater in the all-women workshops. Women are more prone to talk about their personal experiences, while men are much more guarded. We find that men are quite happy to deal with theory, which is abstract and impersonal, but they have little experience of talking about themselves and their emotions. They seem to suffer from the 'brave boy/strong man' syndrome. Men can quite easily talk about the suffering and subordination of poor women, but are not willing to look at their own families. They seem to be trapped in insecurity, based on a fear of the family structure collapsing, and their safe position disappearing from under their feet.

For women, talking about themselves is not only easy: it is a release; because they feel oppressed and do not often get a supportive atmosphere in which to talk about their experiences, they welcome the opportunity. It is much more difficult for men to consider themselves as people who are privileged, who might be oppressing their wives or sisters, consciously or unconsciously, or who might be exploiting the advantages of being men. Although we want the men to talk about themselves as sons, husbands, and fathers, to describe their experiences, to say whether they think they enjoy privileges which their women do not have, to express what they feel about these privileges, and to reflect on the gender differences within the family, somehow the discussions are never really focused or more than superficial. We are not sure whether this is due to lack of time or lack of proper planning, to our own limitations as trainers, or resistance from the male participants. As opposed to this, the personal sessions in women's workshops are very intense and emotional. In almost every session, while talking about the discrimination that they have faced, the oppression or neglect they have suffered, women break down. With women such sessions are often prolonged into the night, but men resist making a shift from the mind to the heart, from the public to the personal. The rare male participant who is willing to explore his personal relationships does not find many male partners and ends up discussing these issues with us women. We have seen three or four men with moist eyes in the last ten years, while innumerable women have wept unabashedly.

Another difference is the men's subtle resistance to thinking about women's subordination as a system. Women, on the other hand, find it very liberating to do so and to name the system. For them this naming of the system, looking at it dispassionately, is the first step towards challenging and dismantling it. This is understandable, because it is in the interest of women to name and change the patriarchal system. This is not so for men, and hence their resistance and defensiveness, especially when it comes to discussing patriarchy in their own, personal context.

Another difference between our workshops with men and those with women is that, in spite of our long experience and abundant grey hair, it is difficult for some men to accept us women as trainers and to admit that we could teach them something. The men who consider themselves leaders are very hesitant to admit that they have not studied or thought seriously about the issue. Some of these men constantly intervene, divert the discussion, and bring in irrelevant issues.

The female facilitators are perhaps always considered to be an 'interested party' in the issue. The fact that it is easier for men to accept male authority became obvious in one of the workshops, when on the fourth day a male guest speaker came and spoke eloquently about religion and culture as the major source of women's oppression. Everyone listened to him in attentive silence, while we women had been heckled for saying things that were only half as radical. Such experiences have made us realise that as women facilitators/trainers we have to learn to use power and authority, use it judiciously, but *use* it. In workshops with women, we never feel the need to use our authority or power; but with men, to be effective and to move the discussions forward, we cannot always reject the use of power completely.

We feel it might be a good idea to have a sensitive male as a co-trainer, someone who can speak 'man to man' with the participants if necessary, and will not be seen as an interested party. Including a man in the trainers' team might blur the divide between men and women that exists when women are trainers and men participants, and the subject being discussed is patriarchy. However, I have conducted all the workshops without a male co-trainer, and in the end all workshops (even those that were tough at first) have been very positive. Except for a couple of men who might have gone away angry, all others have left as friends, even if they did not agree with us completely. The proof of what I am saying is the large number of invitations that I now receive to conduct workshops with senior managers. I have led six workshops each for the senior managers of BRAC and Proshika, three for the entire team of UNFPA, India, two each for UNICEF, Bangladesh and Maldives, three for the partners of SIDA in India, three for the NGO partners of EZE, Christian Aid, ICCO and Bread for the World in India, two in Bangladesh, and others in Pakistan and Sri Lanka.

We need to tread even more gently

We realise that as trainers we have to be much more patient in workshops with men. We should not always speak directly and bluntly, as we do in workshops with women; we should not be confrontational all the time. Much against our nature and thinking, we perhaps have to learn to be circuitous, to take one step forwards and another sideways. After all, the purpose of these workshops is to make allies – not more enemies. Secondly, we must always remember that if for us women developing a feminist understanding and consciousness is a long, painful process, the process of learning and changing will be several times longer and more painful for men. These short workshops are only the first steps of a long journey. But we also realise that, whatever approach we take, there will still be resistance and conflict, especially if we want to discuss personal matters, and if we try to scrutinise family, culture, religion, and language with women's eyes and perspectives.

We feel satisfied with all the workshops we have run. On the whole they have all been positive, and have made enough dents even in those who resist. However, we need to be sensitive to the problems of men who try to break out of their gender roles, to appreciate that they pay a price for it. Unless we are able to feel sympathy for their oppression, without trivialising it by comparing it with women's, we are not likely to go very far in this effort. The problem before us is how to respond to men's oppression seriously and sincerely, without at the same time depoliticising or diffusing the issue of women's subordination. We have no easy answers.

Gender training with men: experiences and reflections from East Africa

Milton Obote Joshua

This seminar gives me an opportunity to appraise the importance of my experience as a male gender-trainer in East Africa. For a good part of the last decade, I have been promoting the principles of gender equality and the empowerment of women – mainly through training and advocacy. From 1992 to 1995, I was part of the original Kenyan gender-training team that was co-ordinated by the African Women's Communication and Development Network, FEMNET-Kenya. From 1996 to the present day, I have been an associate member, trainer, and researcher of the Collaborative Centre for Gender and Development (CCGD). Since 1996, I have also actively participated in the programmes of the Centre for Women Studies and Gender Analysis (CWSGA) of Egerton University, Kenya.

Gender training has arguably been the most widespread activity in the long process of working towards gender equality in Kenya and the East African region, and this is why I am focusing on it here.[1] Before 1991, there was only one East African institution — the Eastern and Southern Africa Management Institute (ESAMI) — that sustained a formal gender-training programme with a high profile. The training module had a strong management orientation, characteristic of ESAMI's mission and vision. From 1990, FEMNET, supported by UNICEF's Kenya Country Office, gradually built up a team of gender trainers, who were drawn from government departments, universities, and the media, as well as some locally based NGOs. This group comprised men and women who had an overt commitment to the promotion of gender equality. This team of gender trainers was seminal in developing gender training as a strategy to promote the principles of equality and equity in Kenya.

In the late 1980s and early 1990s, most initiatives that aimed to redress disparities between women's and men's access to development interventions changed the language of their discourse to that of Gender and Development (GAD). Against this background, gender training in the East African region invariably addresses gender equality from the perspective of women's empowerment. Training objectives are largely guided by the need to promote practices and behaviour which empower women. Most training and advocacy efforts aim to raise the hitherto low status of women in virtually all spheres of life. The achievement of this is contingent upon commensurate changes of attitude and behaviour, particularly from resistant men. The scenarios and arguments in this presentation enable me to shine a spotlight on how male trainers facilitate this change.

I do not want to run the risk of making generalisations about gender training, and am therefore deliberately keeping my focus narrow, concentrating on examining the relative effectiveness of male gender-trainers in breaking male resistance to gender equality. My approach will not be theoretical, and much of what I say has a strong subjective element, but my own point of view is augmented by the experiences, and views, of other trainers and gender experts. These experiences demonstrate that male gender-trainers can play an effective and strategic role in transforming the attitudes of those men who dread the prospect of equality for women.

Gender training: concept and practice in East Africa

Gender training is intended to be a catalytic process, to bring about social transformation of power relations between women and men, at the individual, institutional, and community levels. In order to do this, it is important to recognise that gender issues are inherently 'fluid and situational' (Cornwall and Lindisfarne 1994: 3); gender is a concept that varies according to its cultural context. Therefore, gender training cannot be based on a single, grand 'blueprint' approach. This places considerable demand on trainers to find viable strategies to facilitate social transformation. The necessary concepts, tools, skills, and approaches used will vary, and will evolve in response to constant change in society.

Second, achieving gender equality is impossible without a basic change in people's habits of thought: it requires an awakening or a renewal of the mind. Training that does not recognise this basic fact cannot claim to be contributing towards the principles of fairness and justice for men and women. To the extent that gender trainers respond to diverse training needs, develop modules, and take responsibility for facilitating training sessions, they are a key factor in changing the attitudes and behaviour of people, and bringing about a more gender-sensitive and equal society. In this sense gender training is transformative.

A quick survey of the trends in gender training in the East Africa region reveals three dominant forms of training. First is training *to raise awareness on gender issues*. This level of training aims to transform attitudes towards women and men and their roles in society, and to create an opportunity for gender roles and identities to be recognised as essential elements of a truly human-centred, just, and fair development process. This sensitisation process is the basic level of training. Without this foundation, the second level — that of *gender-analysis skills training* — would be difficult. Training in gender-analysis skills has a technical orientation, in which structured approaches and frameworks are used. These give it a practical relevance in diverse development contexts. The third level of gender training, which is still at a nascent stage, is *gender training for policy analysis and organisational change*. Few organisations are beginning to grapple with the implications of gender equality for organisational policy and practice. Gender training at all three levels is shaped by common social, cultural, and institutional factors. These include common training challenges which hinge upon the dominant patriarchal values that are sustained by the structural and institutional subordination of women.

Despite the emphasis on empowering women, mentioned earlier, in general most initiatives which claim to be based on ideas of Gender and Development (GAD) have remained informed by a Women in Development (WID) approach, focusing on women as a target group, rather than working with both sexes to achieve change. People in East Africa can see that the language might have changed to 'gender equality', but often the discussions still concern women. Gender and Development (GAD) is often perceived as 'women's liberation', disguised as a set of concepts which are supposed to be about both women and men.

Male gender-trainers have had to bear this burden of history. Initially, the response of the public was disparaging, which thwarted our efforts. For example, male trainers were called names and given titles that likened them to women, such as those described in some quarters elsewhere as 'honorary women' (Stacht and Ewing 1997). It is against this background that we should assess the success of male gender-trainers in forming an environment that is more conducive to achieving the aim of equality between women and men.

Methodology and the gender identity of the trainer

Mrs Charity Kabutha, the Program Co-ordinator for Winrock International, East Africa Region (herself an accomplished gender trainer/researcher), points out in an interview that a trainer is not effective simply by being male. He must demonstrate the ability to be practical and tactful in his methodology. He must embrace the principles of adult learning, be flexible without capitulating, be assertive, sensitive, positive, and collaborative, and rely on the workshop approach.[2]

Both male and female trainers are under an obligation to customise training modules and frameworks to meet the needs of trainees, if they are to achieve the degree of practical relevance that it takes to transform habits of mind. Adults learn best when taken through an experiential process. This requires, among other things, that the trainer has the ability to guide a process that relies heavily on practical examples from participants' own situations, and draws out from these examples the need for gender equality. What happens when you plan a gender-training session is that you place a bet on a cluster of activities that you hope will achieve the training objectives. The higher the level of resistance from trainees, the greater the challenge of methodological choices to be made. This is a compelling requirement for the male trainer as well. This way, the trainer's gender becomes an integral factor in the process of making methodological choices.

However, gender training is not a technical issue that is culturally and politically neutral, such as, for example, how to operate a machine. Most of the training designs that I have come across are based on popular frameworks that have been developed for gender analysis. Their potential for changing hearts and minds is always mediated by the manner of their application.

Transformation through training: men's and women's roles

The 'transformative effect' that is the aim of gender training is derived largely from the process through which gender trainers induce discernible change in the views and behaviour of trainees. It can be argued that any male or female gender-trainer can induce changes in the participants' attitudes, as long as he or she is committed to the mission of gender training and has the professional capacity to facilitate participatory and well-informed training programmes. We may say we believe that male trainers may be more effective than female trainers in transforming the attitudes of male trainees, because we are focusing our attention on particular indicators of success, and specific training processes, at the expense of others. We may be giving more attention to the trainer's sex, and to the behavioural and interactive results that we induce in training sessions because of our sex, than we give to other processes at work, and different kinds of competence in the trainer. However, my experience demonstrates that a male trainer does have a higher chance of making men aware of the negative ways in which existing gender relations and stereotypes affect their lives, as well as those of women.

The experience of female and male gender-trainers in East Africa reveals that the prevailing patriarchal social systems in East Africa tend to constrain women's effectiveness. These systems shape society's ideas about how men and women should behave. There is comparatively less acceptance of women's voices in training and advocacy, and wider acceptance of men's claims on these spaces. If this remains the reality of most Eastern African cultures, then the relative effectiveness of male or female gender-trainers depends on what they are perceived to embody and represent in the social order. The implications of this for training are enormous. I now move to examine a few of them.

Gender as a polarising concept

There is a lot of truth in Connell's assertion that a 'gender order where men dominate women cannot avoid constituting men as an interest group concerned with defence, and women as an interest group concerned with change' (Connell 1995: 82). In a sense, this may account for the polarisation between the experiences and interests of women and those of men which has been evident to me in training situations led by a woman. This polarisation is often linked to the cultural construction of men and women as gendered identities. As Hopkins observes, 'man' and 'woman' are 'binary categories, that demand criteria for differentiation' (Hopkins 1998), instead of integration. Social perceptions of men and women seem to follow such differentiation criteria.

However, if we are undertaking training for transformation, we need to question these binary categories, which are so clearly differentiated, by questioning the rationale which shapes our belief that men's and women's identities are inherently different. We say that women and men are 'gendered' through their socialisation. This means that they are often perceived in a stereotypical way, for what they *should* be rather than for what they actually are, and many of us play out stereotypical gender roles in public.

If ideas about gender norms mean that men's domination and control of women, and the 'male' qualities that accompany such domination, are acceptable to any given group, a woman who speaks out assertively will be resented as being a deviant or a misfit who seeks to usurp men's power and control. Her personality and competence as a trainer are ignored, and instead the degree of her conformity or otherwise to the culturally appropriate feminine posture gets more critical attention. This constrains her ability to help men to transform their mentality and attitudes. She enters the training arena defending her position, rather than advancing a case. However, if we are undertaking training for transformation, we need to question these binary categories, which are so clearly differentiated, by questioning the rationale which shapes our belief that men's and women's identities are inherently different.

Man's voice versus woman's voice

'Voice', or the ability to speak, be heard, and listened to, is a powerful tool for asserting control. An important element in men's resistance to women trainers in East Africa is the view that men's voices are more legitimate than women's in public spaces. This belief is rooted in deeply ingrained cultural principles of patriarchy in which the public (community) voice is strategically monopolised by men; one of the most potent strategies of patriarchy is the monopolisation of the public (community) voice by men. Being a man means many things, and the ability to speak openly, with authority and a sense of control, is one of them. Both in the private and in the public spheres, a man's voice carries with it the legitimacy bestowed upon it by culture: a legitimacy that supports and reinforces his status as the rightful leader, spokesperson, and decision maker. A woman's voice is seldom considered legitimate, and is rarely given scope for articulation.

As an example, among the Kikuyu of Kenya, nothing that a woman says in the public domain is to be taken seriously and acted upon immediately. The saying '*cia atumia giti kagio kia rara*' (you sleep over a woman's word) epitomises this point. In other Kenyan communities, such as the Gabra and Samburu, women rarely look directly at men while speaking to them. Instead, they look sideways. Among the Maasai, a woman's voice lacks legitimacy when not sanctioned by male authority. In gender training, a female trainer has a 'less legitimate' voice than the men whom she is training, notwithstanding her education and knowledge. Exceptions are few.

Of course, it is possible for women to find ways around these problems. Selina Nysole, a 24-year-old community mobiliser who worked for a community-development project, called a meeting and was surprised to see Maasai men walking away as soon as she stood to address them. She learned later that the strange behaviour was a reaction to her age and sex. She was told that in Maasai culture, women — especially the young and unmarried — had no powers to address men directly, let alone older men. She also learned that there was cultural provision that could allow her to address men directly in public. All she had to do was to enlist the assistance of the chief to choose a respectable old man from the community. Any time she wanted to address the men, she should stand with the elder next to her. She would address the gathering, and they would then listen, because her voice would be seen to have the authority and legitimacy of the man standing next to her. She complied with this

arrangement, and was surprised at the attention she got from the male-dominated audience (Gender Planning for Community Wildlife Service, staff workshop report, April 1996).

This example highlights a problem common to most cultures: women find themselves unable to articulate issues without reinforcement from men's voice and authority. When they are dealing with gender issues, which are challenging for both women and men, this problem doubles. Women find themselves in a situation with limited or non-existent options, as long as they choose to proceed singly or with other women. In gender training, having women working together with male colleagues provides the necessary counter-balance, as well as reducing resistance to the challenging ideas discussed in gender training. In the case described above, Selina made effective use of culturally sanctioned provisions for women in her situation to address men. To take such an approach may be pragmatic rather than radical, but how long would it take women like Selina to have the right to express themselves and be heard without seeking approval from men? To argue in favour of hearing a male voice in a situation where a female voice is stifled is not to deny that in a truly just society both voices would carry equal weight. The use of a male voice to introduce the message of gender equality should be seen as a necessary first step to get the attention of those who would otherwise not listen in the first place.

Gender as a 'women's issue'

The burden of ignorance about the true meaning of the word 'gender' may be fatal to the effectiveness of female trainers. At the start of training sessions, participants are often invited to share their fears and expectations. This exercise illustrates men's widespread fear of being told about 'women's subordination', 'women's oppression', or 'Beijing domination'. Such fears are indications of the degree to which the concept of gender is misconstrued as a concern only for women. These fears also influence the mental images that the trainees form of the trainers before they even meet them. Thus, you find most participants coming to gender training expecting the trainers to be women. The presence of male trainers provides the initial proof that their fears might just be unfounded. They find their preconceived fears and mental pictures pre-empted, and it is at this point that the trainer can tactfully clarify the fact that gender issues are of practical relevance to both men and women.

Fear of the 'global culture'

Closely related to the last point is the misunderstanding on the part of most East African men that gender and feminism are Western concepts, which are not at all relevant to the African context. Resistance based on this perception echoes Connell's views that 'hard-line masculine fundamentalism goes together with marked anti-internationalism' (Connell 1998: 17). This leads female trainers to be seen as radical, Westernised feminists. It is common for men to point to the female trainer's education, marital status, or manner of dressing as manifestations of her Western and feminist orientation. Surprisingly, I have found that it is the more educated men who entertain this stock perception, in spite of their greater awareness of and exposure to new knowledge and ideas.

Because of such views, trainers of both sexes may be challenged to look for a word from the local language(s) which is equivalent to the English word 'gender'. Beneath this seemingly intellectual and intelligent argument is a strong strategy of denial of gender-based inequality in the African context.

Fear and anxiety over possible loss of power

Most men respond to calls for gender equality from the perspective of their familiar view of the world, and see them as threatening. They see the promise of gender equality in terms of the disintegration of traditional stability and men's power. This fear is compounded by the evidence of negative economic and social change that they see around them in the East African context; for example, growing male unemployment, and loss of secure livelihoods and stable societies. Against this backdrop, efforts to achieve gender equality may be seen as implicated in some elemental driving forces which are challenging men's view of themselves as family providers and breadwinners. It is on these socially designated roles that their superior status has always rested. If men come to gender training with fears like this, they may see transformation as a risk not worth taking, and therefore ignore the messages of the training. A female trainer reinforces this resentment, as she is seen as a characteristic manifestation of the disintegration. Studies have shown elsewhere that most men in such situations become harsh and abusive to women (Barker 1999). They are likely to equate women's advancement with men's dis-empowerment.

Handling culturally sensitive topics

Questions of sexuality and biological reproduction are central to power relations between women and men. We learn from current discourses on masculinity that sexual power, virility, and physical strength are the 'nucleus of masculinity, because they are based on characteristics that are defined as innate and unchangeable' (Fuller 1999: 2). The realisation of masculine power rests on constantly repudiating all that is feminine.

The fact that sexuality is connected to gender-linked power relations means that discussions about it often come up in training situations. It is often very difficult for women to handle sexuality-related topics with a male-dominated audience. When such topics are to be addressed in training, men may be able to handle them with their fellow men with minimal conflict. If one considers this as a purely methodological issue, one might argue that the same applies for women — i.e. it is, similarly, easier for women to handle sexuality issues with other women. While this is true, male gender-trainers can also offer something to women trainees. A male trainer can contend that men use sexuality as a tool for dominating women, and have as a result greater leverage in articulating this point. Men can handle sessions on rape, birth control, sexual behaviour, and ways to improve communication between women and men. The male voice is also relatively more potent in contributing towards controlling and stopping sexual harassment in organisations and society.

Taking a stand

Effective male gender-trainers are those who have taken a stand. They promote gender-equality concerns not as a professional undertaking, but because they believe in the cause and practise the values that underpin such a commitment. Taking a stand brings with it power, integrity, and authenticity. It translates to unlimited possibilities in training situations. Such a trainer is a role model for other men. In a sense, they become 'transparent' in the trainer's presence. They know that the trainer sees them for who they really are. Taking a stand helps to break resistance from doubtful and hostile men. Their indifference and cynicism fade away.

Gender and men's problems

The question of whether or not men's gender-related concerns are taken seriously by development organisations generates a lot of heat whenever it comes up in discussions. I agree with Alversson that taking an interest in gender relations should include taking men more seriously, not just as beneficiaries of patriarchy but also as a broad and divergent category whose members experience mixed feelings, thoughts, and orientations (Alversson 1997: 54). The economically induced decline in men's ability to provide for their families is a gender-based problem which affects men directly, as well as women. The formation in Kenya of an organisation called the Husbands' Support Group (HSG) is one direct result of this trend. The HSG's formation was given impetus by a sense of unease that current social and economic trends — including development interventions — are marginalising men and creating what is termed elsewhere as 'a crisis of masculinity'. It is noteworthy that this organisation draws its membership from highly educated and well-informed men.

Many men respond positively to male gender-trainers in the hope that the male perspective will be highlighted and men's problems emphasised. This reaction is common with men who are fairly well educated and who may be familiar with the dominant discourse on gender. They are men who will argue that gender inequality should end, but that men should not be victims in this process. For every example of the subordination of women, they will have an explanation and countless examples to show that men are not favoured either. Well grounded in the existing literature on the male/female divide, they will introduce and sustain intelligent talk on the origin and basis of gender differentiation. Trainers have to ensure that men see gender inequality in its historical context, as well as in relation to contemporary realities, to discourage exaggerated claims that men are losing out.

Gender training should enable men to recognise that the process of supporting women's empowerment is part of a wide range of strategies for building supportive social systems, and guaranteeing the welfare of households at this time of economic crisis in the region. They should be moved to realise eventually that social and economic reality leaves them with no option but to adapt and co-operate, if they are to play a part with women in building a social system that offers a reliable source of security and stability in the long run.

Diffusing resistance: 'reactive' and 'pro-active' control

Trainers have at their disposal various ways and means of continuously responding to and controlling behaviour that threatens the learning process. In some situations, by simply letting other participants freely argue out a contentious position, the trainer diffuses tension and achieves an adequate measure of control. However, this has not been the case in all situations. Some would argue that the situations that degenerate into conflict and dissent between trainers and participants present challenges that are predominantly methodological.

Techniques of 'reactive control' depend on the image, presence, and active involvement of a facilitator to exert control. Reactive control works best when backed by the trainer's deep knowledge of the subject of gender, and a familiarity with the usual objections raised by resistant participants. Timing is also essential in inducing change in attitudes during training. My own experience in FEMNET, CCGD, and CWSGA, and the experience of colleagues, clearly demonstrates how male trainers can use 'reactive control' in a gender-training situation to counter resistance on the part of male trainees.

We have to recognise that gender training offers a perfect opportunity for men to assert their control over women trainers. One training session in which I was involved in Eastern Kenya was attended by 22 district-level officers (21 male and one female). A male participant raised the issue — more imaginary than real — that in his perception women gender-activists were not only all 'elitists', but also 'social deviants', since they were all unmarried or divorced. What is intriguing about this example is not that this issue came up at all – I find that it usually does. It is rather the manner in which it was used to mobilise spirited resistance to the female trainer. Her voice was lost in unregulated disruptive noise. It was clear that the participants were out to intimidate her and expose her as what they thought she was: namely, someone who, in spite of her education, is a 'social misfit', like all gender activists. One of the two male trainers present was able to stop the din, and proceeded to explain that the allegation was baseless. He did this by citing facts which indicated that the real story about women gender-trainers is very different, while emphasising the need to recognise women and men of all categories as human beings in their own right. The same participants who, minutes before, had been uncontrollable became a relatively obliging audience. In such situations, male trainers can offer effective reactive control. Situations such as this illlustrate the type of occasion when it is viable to use men.

While employing men might have been acceptable, given the time and circumstances of that particular training session, one has to be careful when using a male trainer for reactive control, since his presence may undermine the female trainer and encourage trainees to ignore her. Such interventions by male trainers, and the resulting reaction, risk lending credence to the view — incompatible with gender equality —that only men are capable of addressing men. The Arid and Semi Arid (ASAL) Development Programme in Laikipia district, Kenya, started its training session with male trainers, as a strategy to break resistance from men (predominantly pastoralists). However, staff then realised that it had become difficult to introduce female trainers within the same programme. If sustained, such strategies have the potential to undermine the very rationale for gender training in the first place.

Male trainers are even more effective when they help to achieve control of resistance in a pro-active way. Pro-active control recognises that reactive control comes too late, and that trainers need to anticipate resistance. Male and female trainers working as a team need not wait until cultural resistance to gender equality rears its disruptive head in learning situations. Pro-active control requires having a training strategy and design that can reliably predict what is going to happen, and prepare for it. This is best achieved by undertaking a thorough assessment of training. Using men during the pre-training phase can be instrumental in ensuring that the training gives serious attention to gender issues facing men, and pre-empts resistance from men who have mistakenly regarded gender as an issue for women only. Resistance will not then disrupt the training itself. An assessment of gender-training needs,

conducted by female trainers only, in cultural contexts where women have little public voice, does little to counter such misconceptions and reduce the degree of resistance.

The question of male trainers and objectivity

The use of male gender-trainers has the advantage of objectifying gender issues. I have found that men will admit to a male gender-trainer that women's subordination is a self-evident fact. They will admit this only reluctantly when the issue is raised by a woman. I cannot offer a clear explanation for it, but I would suggest that when a man raises such issues, he is speaking to another man as an equal, and not to one who (in his perception) is laying claim to what she does not have. As such, trainees' attention is directed not towards challenging the facts, but to accepting them as the basis for discussion. This creates a training environment where negotiations may well be positively sustained.

The points highlighted in this section are not intended to undervalue the effectiveness of women as trainers. The instances described here should be seen in the context of the array of tools that trainers should possess, to be able to transform resistant attitudes.

A cautionary tale: the limitations of men as trainers

This section should be read as a cautionary tale about the limitations of men as effective trainers. Above, we have discussed the ways in which male trainers can be effective in breaking men's resistance to gender equality. But male gender-trainers are certainly no panacea for all the problems arising from gender training. As suggested above, experience hows that male gender-trainers may undermine the principles of equality, fairness, and mutual respect between men and women. Ato Shashigo Gerbu, Gender Co-ordinator of the International Institute of Rural Reconstruction (IIRR) in Ethiopia, observes that while men can be effective trainers, they should play only a supportive role. They should be allies rather than commanders in gender training for women's empowerment. Given a chance, he argues, male trainers will establish and/or perpetuate the same kind of exclusive, hierarchical control that gender training seeks to dismantle.

In cultures which have maintained men's voice as the legitimate voice of the community, a male trainer articulates gender issues from a patronising level. His voice lends credence to the unspoken convictions of most men that if women are to be empowered, then men should be the ones to empower them — at their own pace and convenience. Most men consider it safer for a man to articulate gender issues, as he is not expected to undermine the very principles that have given him power and have legitimated his voice. He is a safer option, one whom 'we can work with', and who can be trusted.

Development institutions that are resistant to the promotion of women to senior positions have the greatest tendency to talk about gender as a concept that is not solely about women or solely about men, in order to justify employing men in key positions. One finds the claim that 'women are their own worst enemies' put to effective use in such organisations. By using male trainers, such institutions subtly perpetuate the very basis of inequality, by locking out the women who are disempowered by current gender-linked power relations in the first place. Male trainers cannot in the least be effective this way. Empowering women while retaining control at the level of training excludes and disempowers women.

The majority of men who see in the male trainer a perfect opportunity to delve deeper and exclusively into men's gender concerns reduce the gender problem to mere polemics. They insist on discussing gender as an abstract concept, rather than looking at the impact of unequal power relations on women. If the trainer is not careful, he will find that the training session has been hi-jacked by arguments about the alleged disempowerment of men, even when the reality is otherwise. This kind of subtle resistance amounts to a denial of the fundamental problem. Trainers need to be very familiar with the reality of gender power-relations as they are played out in their particular context, so they can point out real-life situations where inequality prevails.

Another cautionary point is that it is essential to be aware of difference and diversity in any training situation. Many of the points made in this paper so far have related to the fact that the selection of male and/or female trainers is contingent upon having a fair amount of information on the people to be trained: their cultural background, age, language, and perceptions of gender. These are variables that should be known *a priori*, and planned for. They

are essential for the interactions between the trainers and trainees. Ignoring them creates a weak link, especially in situations where training aims to promote women's equality by breaking resistance.

In addition, it is important to recognise that the category of 'men' is not a unitary concept. The world-views of people throughout the East African region are as diverse as they are complex. Because of this, male trainers from a particular cultural background are seldom effective in the same degree in all contexts. Gender equality is contested in varying degrees in different cultures. While I was conducting a gender survey and briefing sessions in Rumbek County, southern Sudan, which is inhabited by the Dinka and Jur communities, I realised that my definition of a man was miles away from theirs. For them, a man is defined in terms of the numbers of wives and cattle he has, and his valour in war, among other things. In that part of Sudan, the on-going civil war appears to have reinforced male supremacy socially and militarily. Gender equality can be seen only within the framework of men as the ultimate wielders of authority. As long as I did not recognise and subscribe to the values that they held so dearly, then I remained an outsider, and the gender-equality messages that I communicated were (at best) foreign and irrelevant.

The last word

I have tried to convey throughout this paper that gender-training sessions are subject to all the same tensions as are present in wider society. Training strategies must address these factors, if positive impact is to be achieved in the post-training period. When resistance manifests itself in the training context, it must not be allowed to multiply and grow. My argument that men are more effective in doing this must be seen as a pragmatic argument only, advanced in the context of my own location at the present time.

That male and female gender-trainers can be allies in undertaking the work of raising awareness and overcoming resistance cannot be gainsaid. Gender training needs diversity in all respects, because it is a fertile ground in which creativity and innovation thrive. Gender training requires innovative approaches. Not least among them is the use of male trainers.

Notes

1   I am grateful to the following trainers and gender experts who shared their views with me as I prepared this paper: Professor Rose Mwonya, Researcher and Gender Trainer, Egerton University, Njoro; Dr Lenha Naknone, Gender Specialist, Egerton University; Mrs Milka Ongayo, PET Consultant; Mr Okumba Miruka, Writer and Training Consultant; Mr Irungu Houghton, Gender Trainer and Senior Advocacy Coordinator, ActionAid Kenya; Mrs Charity Kabutha, Programme Coordinator, Winrock International East African Region; Mrs Yeshi Chiche, Gender Officer, Ethiopia Agricultural Organisation; Mr Shashigo Gerbu, Acting Gender Officer, IIRR Ethiopia; Mr George Karanja, Community Development Officer and Gender Adviser, GTZ/IFSPE Kenya; Mr Wilbert Tengey, Executive Director, Gender Development Institute GDI-Ghana.

2   A lot has been written about the best gender-training approaches. The argument here is based on my practical experience as a trainer in the field, but it is supplemented by: FAO/SEAGA Training Manuals; UNICEF/Bangladesh (1993) *Visualization in Participatory Programmes, VIPP Training Manual*; S. Williams et al. (1995) *The Oxfam Gender Training Manual*; W. Kabira and M. Masheti (1993) *FEMNET Gender Training Model*; and Cummings et al. (1998) *Gender Training: The Source Book*, KIT and Oxfam, among others.

References

Alversson, Ulf and Due Billing (1997), *Understanding Gender and Organisations*, London: Sage.

Barker, G. (1999) 'Masculinity, Identities and Pathways to Manhood', paper presented at the ESRC seminar on Men, Masculinity and Gender Relations in Development, University of East Anglia, 8-9 September 1999.

Connell, R. W. (1995) *Masculinities*, Cambridge: Polity Press.

Connell, R.W. (1998) 'Masculinities and globalization', *Men and Masculinities*, Volume 1, Number 1.

Cornwall A. and N. Lindisfarne (1994) *Dislocating Masculinity*, London: Routledge.

Fuller, N. (1999) 'Masculine Identities Among Peruvian Men', paper presented at the ESRC seminar on Men, Masculinity and Gender Relations in Development, University of East Anglia, 8-9 September 1999.

Greig, A., M. Kimmel, and J. Long (2000) *Men, Masculinities and Development: Broadening Our Work Towards Gender Equality*, UNDP/GIDP Monograph.

Hopkins, Patricia D. (1998) 'Gender treachery, homophobia, masculinities and threatened identities', in Naomi Zack et al. (eds.) *Race, Class, Gender and Sexuality: The Big Question*, Oxford: Blackwell.

Kabira, W. and M. Masheti (1993) 'The FEMNET Gender Training Model', Nairobi: FEMNET.

Stacht, S. P. and D. Ewing (1997) 'The many paths of feminism: can men travel any of them?', *Journal of Gender Studies*.

KIT and Oxfam GB (1998) *Gender Training: The Source Book*, KIT Press and Oxfam GB.

UNICEF/Bangladesh (1993) *Visualization in Participatory Programmes: VIPP Manual*.

Williams, S., J. Seed and A. Mwau (1995) *Oxfam Gender Training Manual*, Oxford: Oxfam.

Male involvement in perpetuating and challenging the practice of female genital mutilation in Egypt

Nadia Wassef

In light of the rising interest in men's roles, it is time for a systematic evaluation of what the prevalent assumptions are about their behaviours, what we actually know about men, and where future studies should be headed.
Greene and Biddlecom (1997)

I saw the razor blade flash after they spilled alcohol on it… I screamed as it burned and tore through my flesh … [She asks] 'Since you love me, why did you sacrifice me?'…'So that men will come running after you without your asking. And when your husband goes away for a long time, you won't suffer at all.'
Alifa Rifaat (1990)

'If this turns out to be a men's liberation movement, I am going to be really annoyed!' my colleague said jokingly. It was during a presentation of some very sketchy ideas for researching the relationship between concepts of masculinity and female genital mutilation (FGM) in Egypt. Three years down the road — research undertaken, report disseminated — her words returned to me. They expressed people's fears, denials, and the general sense of confusion shrouding 'gender' as a category of analysis. In what follows, I discuss the context and factors that led us to shift our attention to men, the areas of contention pertaining to gender, and the findings that emerged from this study. Throughout the twentieth century, FGM-eradication campaigns in Egypt had been sporadic. Adopting various strategies, they ranged from barely coping with the existence of the practice to actively resisting its perpetuation (Wassef 1998). The focus of the 1994 UN International Conference on Population and Development (ICPD) on issues of reproductive health placed FGM at the forefront of attention. After much discussion and negotiation, the Egyptian Female Genital Mutilation Task Force was created, under the umbrella of the National NGO Commission on Population and Development (NCPD), with the responsibility of following up the ICPD recommendations. In the years that followed, the Task Force — comprising 'organisations and individuals, women and men, active in several fields of development: women's rights, health, human rights, education and legal aid' — employed multiple strategies to address the issue of FGM (FGM Task Force 1997: 1). We identified, researched, and addressed various target groups. In charting different approaches for engaging in discussions and advocacy campaigns in local communities and with decision-makers, we sought dialogues with various sectors of the population.

Our protean structure reflected an eclectic synthesis of tools and approaches. A favoured approach among activists working against the practice emphasised the negative side-effects of FGM. Addressing women by telling them of the risk of haemorrhage, pain, and trauma elicited mixed feedback. Although an effective way of shocking people into stopping the practice, it was also an exercise in 'latent threats', in the sense that activists were saying, 'If you do this, then the following disasters will ensue.' Working against this message were those circumcised women whose health had not suffered and who could allay the fears of others. Two consequences unfolded. First, those who did not suffer during the procedure easily contested activists' stress on the health message, which reduced the credibility of the latter. Second, highlighting the context of the operation and the medical aspects of it led to a discussion of medicalisation, rather than eradication. The discussion revolved around who should perform FGM and where, rather than questioning the rationale for practising it in the first place. People believed that they could continue practising FGM, as long as it was performed in a hospital or clinic where modern medicine could cater for any eventuality. By the 1990s, the FGM Task Force realised the need for other approaches, to reduce the emphasis on health. Focusing on rights, development, and gender offered means of involving new actors. This was no longer a discussion between health workers, activists, and mothers about the futures of their daughters.

Men: the absent/present

In 1995, the Egyptian Demographic and Health Survey revealed that 97 per cent of women currently married or widowed had been circumcised (EDHS 1995: 171). In this light, the entire population, with the exception of a few positive deviants, emerged as our target audience. More research ensued. Religious officials, community leaders, teachers, doctors, and mothers surfaced as objects of study. Conspicuous by their absence were half the population: men. In research with the said target groups, men were addressed, but as makers of public opinion and respected figures in the community who could sway others. They were never perceived as fathers, husbands, sons, and brothers of circumcised women, with a direct involvement in the practice. The public persona was divorced from the personal self by an artificial boundary.

Men surfaced as the 'absent/present' in studies assessing knowledge about, attitudes to, and practice of FGM in Egypt. In the rare instances when they were directly questioned about FGM, they were addressed in their capacity as public figures. Women's words hinted at their indirect presence. Men's assumed needs and expectations of women predominated as frames of reference when exploring rationales for the practice. The EDHS reaffirmed what other studies preceding it had suggested: the perceived needs of men directly and indirectly motivated the practice of FGM. Of the 14,779 respondents, 8.9 per cent cited 'better marriage prospects', 5.6 per cent 'prevention of adultery', and 3.8 per cent 'the greater pleasure of the husband' as reasons in support of practising circumcision (EDHS 1995: 173). In Alifa Rifaat's short story, *Who Will Be The Man?* (1990), the mother's words to her daughter, quoted above, echoed these reasons. The most commonly cited reason — 'good tradition' — that featured in 53.8 per cent of the respondents' answers indirectly implicated men. Male involvement manifests itself in the relationships between women's bodies and tradition within the context of patriarchal societies (Kandiyoti 1991).

Men's roles as breadwinners and decision makers influenced their daughters' fates. One study indicated that in the event of a man's absence from the nuclear family, or when the wife enjoys a measure of financial independence, the daughter has a higher chance of remaining uncircumcised (Badawi in Hosken 1993). During focus-group discussions with men in various Egyptian governorates, female participants said that men had the final say on all matters pertaining to the family, even FGM, which contradicted assumptions that more 'personal' matters were left to the mother's discretion (El-Katsha *et al.* 1997). Other arguments cited the father's role in paying for the circumcision, and the gifts and celebrations that accompany it (Constantinides 1985). Men's ubiquitous roles were inversely proportional to the research that addressed them. As much as their involvement in the practice seemed pivotal, they were hardly given a passing glance by researchers, policy planners, and development practitioners.

Diverting the female gaze: looking at men in Egypt

Egypt's specific experience of the paradigmatic shifts from WiD/WaD (women in/and development) to GaD (gender and development) as categories of analysis explained the emergence and inclusion of men within development and feminist perspectives. In 1975, the start of the United Nations decade for women, the notion of 'empowerment' was emphasised. More than two decades later, the shortcomings of the methods and formulations employed in this focus on women crystallised. One way of summing up the activist position in Egypt is to question the point and the efficacy of literacy classes, legal-rights awareness raising, and health and family-planning campaigns, and to highlight the lack of political participation for women when their fathers, husbands, brothers, and sons remain oblivious to these endeavours or their necessity. Aren't these men part of the same society? Don't women have to negotiate with them? Isn't FGM itself a manifestation of the patriarchal bargain that women strike at the expense of their bodies? This realisation prompted an embrace of the concept of gender equity, with its rhetorical promises of inclusion. The New Woman Research Centre, an Egyptian women's rights organisation, exemplified this sentiment in one of its posters, which read: '*Women's Liberation is Men's Liberation*'.

Even when activists and academics embraced gender as a category of analysis, that still did not guarantee the inclusion of men as subjects of research. Until recently, most research in the fields of anthropology, development, demography, and women's studies, when speaking of gender, focused solely on women. An example from demography demonstrates the persistence of the problem: 'while the term gender has gained in popularity, often it is invoked when what is actually being addressed is the biological category of sex' (Greene and Biddlecom 1997: 10). This myopic view resulted in a pervasive *politics of gynocentrism*. With reference to FGM, statements describing the practice as 'an act of violence perpetrated by women against women' went unchecked. Women were at once the perpetrators and victims of this practice. But what of men? The formulation of the issue in these terms obliterates their presence, interests, and power. On the level of discourse, the repercussions are dire. FGM and violence against women are represented as women's issues, which produces a distorted view of them, as well as a monopoly of women working on them. This is reflected in, and reaffirmed by, men's absence in research into those topics. In the words of Greene and Biddlecom (1997: 3):

'The assumption of women's primacy in fertility and contraceptive use has led to a general downplaying and often neglect of men's roles in studies of fertility and family planning. While conception necessarily requires two participants, demographic studies of family planning, and especially fertility, historically focused solely on women because of an overarching interest in outcomes, i.e., the actual number of babies, who, after all, emerge only from women's bodies.'

The outcome is a highly polarised debate, revolving around certain binary oppositions: male/female, production/reproduction, and public/private (Ali 1998). People's realities are seldom so clearly delineated, and the attempt to tidily schematise them reinforces the use of false terms in an unnecessarily polarised debate.

The influence of the ICPD on development policy and practice in Egypt was pivotal in the realisations that it prompted. Women's reproductive health was now on the agenda, with all its far-reaching implications. In the section entitled 'Gender Equality, Equity, and Empowerment of Women' in the *Program of Action*, the following position regarding men was put forward.

Male responsibilities and participation

Men play a key role in bringing about gender equality since in most societies they exercise preponderant power in nearly every sphere of life. The objective is to promote gender equality and to encourage and enable men to take responsibility for their sexual and reproductive behaviour and their social and family roles. Governments should promote equal participation of women and men in all areas of family and household responsibilities … and shared control in and contribution to family income and children's welfare (Program of Action 1995: 10).

This document affirmed men's involvement in most aspects of women's issues. The challenge was to convince them of this and to secure their participation in achieving change. This in itself was highly problematic, since most men and women in the FGM studies previously referred to were oblivious of the degree of men's involvement.

'Gender' emerged as the all-encompassing term under whose rubric relations between men and women could be analysed and discussed. Improving on its predecessor — Women and Development (WAD) — the Gender and Development framework worked towards 'upsetting the existing power relations in society between men and women' (Visvanathan 1997: 19). Before discussing the emphasis on gender — and, by extension, men — in Egypt, I will discuss a few theoretical problems and concerns implied by the concept. In exploring waves of feminisms over the last century in the Middle East and the West, Deniz Kandiyoti linked post-structural and post-modern debates with 'a gradual but significant shift from "woman" to "gender" (Kandiyoti 1996: 6). Feminists challenged the idea of woman as a monolithic entity. Oppression cannot be explained through a unifying all-encompassing grand narrative. This deconstruction of the category of 'woman' led to an emphasis on plurality and power relations (Butler 1990). Decades earlier, Simone de Beauvoir's celebrated utterance, *'One is not born a woman, but rather becomes one'*, signalled the rise of the concept of gender (de Beauvoir 1988: 295). Since then, feminists have elaborated this insight to encompass a plethora of ideas.

The concept of gender thus provides an overarching rubric for looking at historical, cultural, and situational variability in the definitions of womanhood and manhood, in meanings of masculinity and femininity, in relationships between men and women, and in the extent of their relative power and political status ... it is never fixed, but rather is continually constituted and reconstituted. (Glenn 1999: 5)

This entailed an examination of how all aspects of human relationships, institutions, cultures, and societies are gendered. Although the focus on gender signalled the move away from woman and the body (which relied on concepts of sex and biological determinism), it remains problematic, since it is premised on the very assumption that it was supposed to nullify.

... the sex/gender distinction suggests a radical discontinuity between sexed bodies and culturally constructed genders ... The presumption of a binary gender system implicitly retains the belief in a mimetic relation of gender to sex whereby gender mirrors sex or is otherwise restricted by it ... the radical splitting of the gendered subject poses yet another set of problems. Can we refer to a 'given' sex or a 'given' gender without first inquiring into how sex and/or gender is given, through what means? ... It would make no sense, then, to define gender as the cultural interpretation of sex, if sex itself is a gendered category. (Butler 1990: 6-7)

For our purposes, sex and gender are 'organisations of perception rather than transparent descriptions or reflections of nature' (Scott 1999: 73). I need a category of analysis through which to organise perceptions, and gender currently suits those needs. Perhaps at this juncture, a further split occurs between the agendas and outlooks of activists and academics.

The animosity — or, more mildly put, ambivalence — towards gender emanated from those who were uncomfortable with restructuring the field to encompass the study of men and masculinities. In her review of this debate, Kandiyoti illustrates this point by reminding us that gender was at times referred to as 'new men's studies' (Kandiyoti 1996: 6). Activists in Jamaica and Bangladesh echoed this protest against the use of gender as a category in development, because it focused on men and denied women's problems (Baden and Goetz 1998). While this is an experience and concern shared by other activists and scholars internationally, the situation in the development field in Egypt is different.

Let me make my position clear: for the purposes of research in the field of development, I support the use of gender as a category of analysis. I have found it helpful, despite its theoretical limitations. But there are certain problems that must be addressed regarding this term. The main one is that it has come to mean so many different things to different factions, depending on the context. Scholars such as Butler reached an impasse with the term and found that it was not so different from notions of sex difference (which it is supposed to refute). Some activists criticised this dilution of feminism, while others welcomed this shift as a way of making women's issues and agendas more accessible to men, and less threatening to society in general. Answering one question would assist in clarifying these issues: *why are we studying men?* Once this hurdle is overcome, the focus and aims of our work become clearer.

Making some decisions

In this section, I examine problematic elements in the study of men, using my research conducted at the behest of the FGM Task Force on masculinity and FGM in Egypt as an example (Wassef and Mansour 1999). This study was the result of two simultaneous events: the paradigmatic shifts that led to the adoption of gender as a tool of analysis, and the realisation that the medical approach in FGM-eradication efforts was too narrow, and that different target groups should be addressed, using wider approaches to the problem. In the ICPD recommendations, men are construed as the gatekeepers of women's empowerment, since they 'exercise preponderant power in nearly every sphere of life' (*Program of Action* 1995: 10). In the instance of demography men are important, since they are the context of women's negotiations. We can surmise that the study of men in these circumstances is informed by a desire to assist women. Paying attention to men is merely a detour en route to attaining the real objective of the exercise. Within this equation they emerge as women's accessories (at best), or as obstacles to the attainment of the ultimate goal.

In examining the relationship between feminism and anthropology, the attempt to include women as objects of study could not be done through the 'add-women-and-stir method' (Moore 1988: 3). The endeavour necessitated an on-going revisioning of agendas, goals, and methodologies. The same

47

applies to the study of men and masculinity. Adding men and stirring the mixture produces flat and superficial results. Just as 'feminist anthropology is not, therefore, about "adding" women into the discipline, but is instead about confronting the conceptual and analytic inadequacies of disciplinary theory', the study of men requires no less (Moore 1988: 4). In studying men, we should question what is meant by the homogeneous term 'men'. Having subjected the category of 'women' to deconstruction, the category of 'men' demands similar interrogation. 'By looking in detail at everyday usage and the contexts in which people talk of masculinity, its complexity soon becomes apparent' (Cornwall and Lindisfarne 1994: 2).

Given my commitment to women's rights, my involvement in campaigns against FGM, and my readiness to look to men as a new target group and as allies in a struggle, a few decisions had to be made in a study of masculinity and FGM. Just as those embarking on the 'anthropology of women' were aware of the various levels of male bias (Moore 1988: 1), I and my male research assistant were grappling with the feminist bias that we brought to our work. While a surface reading of FGM implies that it is a practice performed by women on other women's bodies, we felt that it could be read as a language inscribed on the female body that offered clues about men. Our intention was not to suggest that women's bodies mirrored men's anxieties, but to look at a more subtle and complex web of relationships and assumptions that led to and reinforced the practice of circumcision.

Were we studying men for their own sake, or were they mere accessories to the central figures — women? Men were the objects of our study, which sought entry points and areas of engagement with them in the struggle against FGM. Men's relationship to FGM served as the defining line. Unlike instances in demography and fertility studies, where the inclusion of men extended only to assessing their involvement in their spouse's use of contraceptives, in the case of FGM the issue was properly understood in relation to a wider spectrum of concerns. During the in-depth, one-to-one, loosely structured interviews that we conducted, we posed one question about FGM. Discussions of concepts of masculinity, understandings of a healthy sex life, sexuality, and women dominated the remainder of the lengthy interviews. How did our respondents perceive women? What were their attitudes to sex? How did they conceptualise women in their fantasies? What were their understandings and expectations of marriage? What were their attitudes to children? How did they feel about impotence? It was only through posing broad questions that we were able to establish specific links between the issue of FGM and men's attitudes, anxieties, and expectations about women, marriage, and themselves. Many levels of perception and experience had to be explored in an effort to understand the complexities of male identities. This research took men as its objects of study, with the goal of improving the lives of men and women. Above all we emphasised the *politics of the particular* in the study of men, favouring fragmented 'masculinities'.

Complex relationships: men, masculinities, mutilations

After more than sixty hours of taped interviews with men of varying ages, marital status, and education levels, we were ready to start data analysis. Having opted for a qualitative approach to our data, I was extremely conscious of being a feminist engaged in analysing men's words. Would my own biases lead the direction of this research astray? The impact of a researcher's gender on his or her fieldwork is inescapable. 'We do fieldwork by establishing relationships, and by learning to see, think and be in another culture and we do this as persons of a particular age, sexual orientation, belief, educational background, ethnic identity and class' (Bell 1993: 1-2). After writing countless drafts 'situating' myself within the project for the purposes of transparency and reflexivity, I began the data analysis.

Our original set of questions led to the discussion of semi-related issues that included domestic violence, women's materialism, men's vulnerability, adultery, impotence, and religious teaching on sex. In general, our respondents avoided speaking in particulars and were more comfortable when referring to what 'others' did and thought. As the interviews progressed, they slipped into talking about themselves. In discussions of information about sex, most of the sample reported receiving their limited knowledge through 'unofficial' channels such as friends, pornographic magazines, insults, and (for those in the countryside) observing animals. Attempts to ask fathers, teachers, and other repositories of 'legitimate knowledge' were met with two words that silenced the youths: *haram* (forbidden) and *'aib* (disgraceful). Even more problematic is the fact that men in our sample who have children of their own repeat the same behavioural patterns, choosing to keep them in the dark. Sayed said, '*I never asked my father, I couldn't. And I can't tell my children either. My son can learn about sex spontaneously, or through jokes.*'

Our respondents' understanding of masculinity (*rugula* in Arabic, which connotes masculinity, virility, and manhood) oscillated between the sexual and the social. In defining this notion, older men emphasised actions and behaviours within the community, while younger men located *rugula* in the body and through sexual potency. Medhat, from the middle age-bracket, illustrated this shift: '*Masculinity is the ability to deal with my life, marry, provide for my home, work, and conceive. Previously, I thought that it was to smoke and have sex.*' Masculinity was not intrinsically given at birth, but an ideal that one must assert and work towards, since it existed only when exercised upon others. In this light, sex surfaced as an important vehicle of domination. Taher felt that one of the defining strains of masculinity was '*to be stronger than the woman*'. While most men initially hesitated in equating masculinity with sexual potency, when presented with the scenario of a man who was a breadwinner and pillar of the community, but impotent, they deemed him to be lacking in *rugula*, despite the primacy accorded to financial autonomy and social standing.

Impotence for most of the sample was a fate worse than death. Respondents felt that in the event of experiencing sexual weakness, the honourable man would offer his wife a divorce. For in the long run, women could not live without sex and would inevitably sin, thus bringing shame on to their families. I cannot emphasise enough the importance and anxiety expressed by our respondents with regard to this issue. When asked about Viagra, most of the sample felt that it was acceptable for a man to take it, since that would guarantee the stability of his marriage and his life. Seen in the light of these anxieties, FGM operates in an inversely proportional way to Viagra and serves as a pre-emptive strike that enhances the men's confidence in their masculinity. FGM weakens women, and Viagra empowers men, turning the odds in men's favour (Wassef 1999). Also noteworthy were the constant references to women's sexual rights within marriage. As far as respondents were concerned (with the exception of one), these were the only rights that were mentioned in association with women.

Men felt themselves to be at a disadvantage, because women understood and could manipulate them more than they could women. The images of women that our respondents offered ranged from obsessive materialism to nymphomania. The perceptions of women's needs in a man ranged from sensitivity at one extreme to Herculean strength at the other. Maged felt that '*women like rough men*'; Abdelrahman elaborated that, suggesting '*a man who can beat up other men*'. It was tacitly understood that women derived their power in the eyes of others from the power wielded by their men. It was assumed that women liked men who showed them that they were in charge and could dominate them sexually and financially. These conventional images reflect mutually exclusive, unrealistic, and unsophisticated categories of masculinity and femininity. Yet our respondents shared similar views and anxieties. Even when their realities contested these stereotypes, our respondents still chose to believe in abstract generalisations.

Using these ideas as a frame of reference against which we can understand FGM produces a more complex picture. Most of our respondents could not give us accurate information about what FGM was, other than the removal of '*something from down there*'. They had very strong views about the desirability of marrying circumcised women and circumcising their daughters. Guaranteeing less excitable and less demanding women, in the minds of these men, ensured better futures for all involved — and they knew that FGM could deliver this. The men who did not circumcise their daughters, like Lotfi, gave reasons such as: '*I have had sex with both types [circumcised and uncircumcised], and honestly there is no difference.*' Opposing this view, Medhat believed that FGM was done to '*avoid friction between the girl and her clothes, which increases her lust*', and Hassan affirmed that FGM '*makes a man happier*'. Most respondents advocated FGM for their social dependants (wife, daughter, and sister), but were adamantly against it for a woman with whom they might have an extra-marital affair.

Respondents opposed to the practice had various rationales for their positions. Maher cited a number of reasons:

No one has the right to deprive anyone of their will ... no one has the right to stifle someone ... it is not proven that female circumcision protects the girl from anything ... it is also a violation. You have to give the girl her freedom. A person who takes the decision to circumcise a girl, regardless of whether it is the father or mother, is a thief who is stealing the girl's will ... I didn't want to marry a circumcised woman ... I don't want an incomplete person physiologically or psychologically.

Mohsen attacked the supposition of FGM's ability to prevent adultery: '*Women don't cheat on men easily ... female circumcision is not going to stop it ... castrate your friend, so he won't betray you with your wife.*' Akram's regret at circumcising his oldest daughter ensured that her siblings were spared:

I have never tried an uncircumcised woman ... and they say it's better to stick with what you know. Maybe out of curiosity I would like to marry an uncircumcised woman. I would be scared ... at this age I can't take an uncircumcised woman ... I circumcised my daughter unfortunately ... I was taken by surprise ... her mother's mother did it ... every time I remember that instant, I hate myself. My daughter told me 'aib ya baba ... because I delivered her to another person ... I now know it is not demanded by religion ... you raise them, teach them, direct them and the mother is good ... then the girl will be clean.

Akram was one of the few men who looked at the issue of FGM from the girl's perspective. For him and many of the other respondents, these interviews were the first time they had been asked to articulate, explain, and defend their positions. In some cases, they were not as sure of their opinions and perceptions of the world as they had been at the outset.

Our recommendations tried in a gender-sensitive manner to address the anxieties and practices raised in the interviews. Initially, we decided to begin the dissemination phase by sharing our findings with community-based organisations and asking men and women to react to our data. Seeking a partnership, in the form of a dialogic interaction, led to asking men from these organisations to draft the recommendations that they wanted. This study already pushed for undertaking further research, using different foci and methods. On the awareness-raising front, we emphasised family communication as a value, and the glorification of fatherhood, and called for gender-sensitive sex education. We would also like to see a series of discussion groups and pamphlets for use in local communities, introducing men to women's rights and women's issues, as well as the dissemination of specific information on FGM tailored to men. In this vein, we also encourage the publication and dissemination of men's testimonies regarding their experiences of FGM, whether in their relationships to their wives or to their children.

Our study changed the attitudes of the men whom we interviewed, by demystifying and questioning the preconceived notions that governed their lives. At the same time, it reaffirmed our belief in using gender as a category of analysis. Clearly, however, it is a category that must be re-appropriated every time it is used, to suit the context in which it is invoked. Gender does not mean women. In the case of FGM, gender is being re-moulded to include not only 'women's issues' but also power relations between men and women, relations that operate at all levels of society and its institutions. Men are involved in FGM — both directly and indirectly: it is insufficient simply to assume that FGM 'somehow' makes men more secure in their masculinity. In order to enhance the efficacy of development work, a more nuanced and balanced approach is required, one in which the use of gender as a category of analysis focuses on the needs of both women and men, to the exclusion of none and to the greater benefit of all.

References

Ali, K. A (1988) 'Planning the Family: Some Thoughts on Research on Egyptian Men and Women', unpublished paper presented at a seminar entitled 'Research on Male Involvement in Reproductive Health in Egypt', Alexandria, 4-5 May 1988.

Baden, S. and A. Goetz (1998) 'Who needs [sex] when you can have [gender]? Conflicting discourses on gender at Beijing', in *Feminist Visions of Development: Gender Analysis and Polity*, edited by C. Jackson and R. Pearson, London: Routledge.

de Beauvoir, S. (1988) *The Second Sex*, H.M. Parshley (trans.), London: Picador. First published in 1949.

Bell, D. (1993) 'Introduction' in *Gendered Fields: Women, Men and Ethnography*, edited by Diane

Bell, Pat Caplan, and Wazir Jahan Karim, London: Routledge.

Butler, J. (1990) *Gender Trouble: Feminism and the Subversion of Identity*, New York: Routledge.

Constantinides, P. (1985) 'Women heal women: spirit possession and sexual segregation in a Muslim society', *Social Science Medicine*, Vol. 21, No.6.

Cornwall, A. and N. Lindisfarne (1994) 'Dislocating masculinity: gender, power and Anthropology', in *Dislocating Masculinity: Comparative Ethnographies*, edited by A. Cornwall and N. Lindisfarne, London: Routledge.

Egyptian Demographic and Health Survey (1995), Cairo: National Population Council, Calverton, Md.: Macro International.

El-Katsha, S., S. Ibrahim, and N. Sedky (1997) *Experiences of Non-Governmental Organisations Working Towards the Elimination of Female Genital Mutilation in Egypt*, Cairo: CEDPA and ESPD.

FGM Task Force (1997) *FGM Task Force Position Paper*, Cairo.

Glenn, E. N. (1999) 'The social construction and institutionalisation of gender and race: an integrative framework', in *Revisioning Gender*, edited by Myra Marx Ferree, Judith Lorber, and Beth B. Hess, London: Sage Publications.

Greene, M. E. and A. E. Biddlecom (1997) 'Absent and Problematic Men: Demographic Accounts of Male Reproductive Roles', *Working Papers*, No. 103, Population Council: Policy Research Division.

Hosken, F. (1993) *The Hosken Report*, 4th edition, Lexington, MA: WIN NEWS. Kandiyoti, D. (1991) 'Introduction' in *Women, Islam and the State*, London: Macmillan.

Kandiyoti, D. (1996) 'Contemporary feminist scholarship and Middle East studies', in *Gendering the Middle East: Emerging Perspectives*, edited by Deniz Kandiyoti, Syracuse: Syracuse University Press.

Moore, H. (1988) *Feminism and Anthropology*, Cambridge: Polity Press.

Program of Action of the 1994 International Conference on Population and Development (1995), Chapter IV, 'Gender equality, equity, and empowerment of women'.

Rifaat, A. (1990) 'Who will be the man?' (1981), in *Opening the Gates: A Century of Arab Feminist Writing*, edited by M. Badran and M. Cooke, London: Virago.

Scott, J. W. (1999) 'Some reflections on gender and politics' in *Revisioning Gender*, edited by Myra Marx Ferree, Judith Lorber, and Beth B. Hess, London: Sage Publications.

Visvanathan, N. (1997) 'Introduction to Part 1', in *The Women, Gender, and Development Reader*, edited by N. Visvanathan, L. Duggan, L. Nisonoff, and N. Wiegersma, London: Zed Books.

Wassef, N. (1998) *Da Min Zaman: Munadharat al-Mady wa'l-Hadir Hawl al-Tashweeh al-Ginsy lil-Inath fi Misr* (Past and Present Discourse on FGM in Egypt), Cairo: Friedrich Ebert Stiftung.

Wassef, N. (1999) 'Asserting masculinities: FGM in Egypt revisited' in *Association for Middle Eastern Women's Studies Review*, Vol. 14, No. 3.

Wassef, N. and A. Mansour (1999) *Investigating Masculinities and Female Genital Mutilation*, Cairo: National NGO Centre for Population and Development.

Men's roles, gender relations, and sustainability in water supplies: some lessons from Nepal

Shibesh Chandra Regmi and Ben Fawcett

There is a tendency among agencies engaged in installing water supplies in Nepal to claim that their drinking-water projects can deliver sustainable practical benefits to women and men in the project communities. Study of the water-supply interventions of some agencies, including non-governmental, bilateral, and government organisations, carried out from a gender perspective in various regions of Nepal over a period of two years (early 1997 to early 1999), shows different results. One major finding of the research is that, despite the importance of women's strategic involvement in the management of water supplies, as highlighted by the literature on gender and development, the drinking-water sector still appears insensitive to gender issues in Nepal. The following discussions support this finding.

Token involvement of women in community water projects

In all the agencies studied, the technicians carrying out the feasibility study and planning, designing, and implementing water projects are men. Assuming that the local men have more spare time than women, these male technicians contacted more men than women to participate in various project activities, in order that the project works could be finished on time. As a result, only the local men were involved in the important phases of the project. For example, men make major decisions related to the location of tube-wells or tap-stands, and the selection of caretakers or maintenance workers, skilled workers and contractors, candidates for training courses, and membership of the water committees and various user groups. The male technicians' understanding of women's participation in project activities is limited to the presence of a few women on water committees and in user groups, and the presence of relatively more women in community meetings, while the technicians perceive men as the principal decision-makers, both in the household and the project.

For example, in Hile village in east Nepal, the two women on the local water committee reported that they had not known for months that they had been selected by the local men to serve on the committee. Because the male committee members had been instructed by the project officials to include two women in the committee, they had put the women's names forward as a token, in order to activate the implementation of the water project. These women said that because the men involved them only in order to meet the project requirement, they were not consulted either by the male technicians or by the male committee members when any decisions were made. They also said that they were not invited to participate in meetings, nor were they included on the sub-committee, composed entirely of men, that was formed to monitor the project's progress.

The impact of water projects on women's daily lives

On the other hand, the contacts (however limited) between the male staff of the projects and the local men involved during the negotiation stage can lead to many negative consequences, although they claim that their aim is to improve women's lives. One such consequence is worth sharing here. In all the communities studied, women complained that their water-collection time had increased significantly (sometimes as much as four or five times) after the improved water services had been installed. This is in part because the tap-stands and tube-wells are located along the road side, where they cannot bathe freely nor easily wash the clothes that they use during menstruation, for fear of being seen by males. In order to avoid this, women in Hile village in east Nepal (which is in the hills and has a cold climate) carry water all the way to their homes several times each day, expending significant amounts of energy to do so. In three villages on the Tarai plain (Motipur, Magaragadhi, and Gajedi) in west Nepal, women reported waiting

52

until dark to undertake these activities. They said that they had not had this problem when they had used more distant traditional sources, where there was no chance of men being around.

Despite the claim of some of the projects to improve the lives of women by reducing their work burden, it was found that their workload had actually increased. Although the projects have made water services more accessible than before, the local men (who have more free time than the women) have not yet started sharing women's responsibility for water-hauling, which in Tarai has increased tremendously, owing to the greater use of water by family members in a majority of households. The research findings show that women in the communities selected for study work up to 18 hours a day, while men work up to 13 hours. Apart from ploughing, there is hardly any regular activity that is performed exclusively by men; but there are many that are exclusively female. In their supposed rest hours, men spend time drinking and playing cards, while women knit, sew, and weave. Men expressed the view that their agricultural work (mainly ploughing and preparing the fields) was much harder than that of women. In fact, not only do women work longer hours, but some of their activities, such as collecting fuel, fodder, and water, are at least as labour-intensive as men's work in the fields. In all communities, the women reported that they used to collect water four to five times a day, amounting to a total of 80 litres per family per day. But after water was supplied nearer their homes, they fetched water 10–15 times, with households using as much as 200–300 litres of water a day.

Exclusion of women from project management

Because the male technicians made no attempt to understand the gender roles, gender relations, and the factors affecting those roles and relationships in order to devise ways to mobilise both women and men effectively in various project activities, it was only men who found time to participate in the project. For example, two women members of the water-users' committee in Gajedi village in west Nepal reported that they had attended only one out of ten local committee meetings held in the previous year, because the meeting place was too far away and there was no one to share their work at home. They said that, although their husbands supported the idea of their participation in such meetings, the men failed to realise that this would be impossible if they did not share the domestic work. These women suggested that the projects should focus more on how to motivate men to share women's work, rather than spending time on trying to involve women in project activities, since their involvement is never meaningful without men's sincere cooperation.

The other issue of concern is that all the male project staff in the selected projects seemed to think that men, in general, are the breadwinners, are more capable than women of doing labour-intensive work, and more suited than women to technical tasks. This leads them to suggest that it is men who should receive technical training and payment for their work. So the selected projects provided technical training exclusively to men, and recruited men as paid workers and women mainly as volunteers. Even in the few cases where both women and men were recruited for daily wage-labour activities, men were paid a little higher than women. This happened, for example, during the construction phase of the Hile drinking water project. The argument was that men work harder than women and thus they should be paid more. Since the project staff were all men, they agreed with the local men's argument and paid them more than women. On the other hand, women labourers said that men should in fact have been paid less than them, as they spent time chatting and smoking cigarettes, in contrast to the women, who, they argued, were very dedicated to their work.

This male bias is seen not only at the community level but also at the organisational level. In all selected organisations, more men than women are hired in general, and especially to perform the technical tasks that yield more income. Even when women are hired as technicians, only men are sent to do the field jobs, on the basis that the field work is labour-intensive and thus beyond the women's capacity. An example comes from the government district water-supply office in Dhankuta, eastern Nepal, where three women were recruited as water supply and sanitation technicians. However, senior officers decided that women cannot undertake labour-intensive activities in the field, and so these employees have been reassigned to perform administrative tasks.

The implication is that, although the projects claim that their improved water services can enhance the quality of the lives of women, they have actually had a greater positive impact on the lives of men. In other words, men's bargaining power is now even higher than before, even though women are investing a significant amount of their time in the project activities.

Male bias in the sharing of benefits

The research project studied the issue of equity in the sharing of project benefits. The men who dominated both the agencies and the communities could not figure out, while conceptualising, designing, and implementing projects, whether the benefits of the projects would be equally shared by all users in the communities. Questions of gender, caste, ethnicity, and class were all overlooked. For example, the amount of cash to be contributed to meet the capital costs and the operational and maintenance costs was decided by men, although this responsibility actually fell on women, as the primary users of water resources. Because men mostly control household incomes, women face difficulties in paying the water tariffs. Consequently the number of women defaulters has increased, raising a doubt about whether they will be allowed continued access to the improved water resources. For example, in one meeting about the collection of the water tariffs in Gajedi village, it was found that the tariffs were mostly paid by women, and that women from female-headed households were among the defaulters. A decision was taken in the meeting that if the defaulters did not pay their dues within 15 days, they would not be allowed to use the tube-wells. Two of the defaulters contacted for further investigation, who were very poor and lived a hand-to-mouth existence with their two to three children, were very shocked by this decision of the committee. They did not know what they would do if they were banned from using the tube-well. The danger in such a case is that these households may revert to using unhygienic water sources, risking the health of everyone in the family.

Moreover, because the male technicians had chosen to limit their contact with the local women, the women in households whose men were temporarily or permanently absent could not voice their concerns during the planning stage. Such women, who are mostly from lower caste/ethnic groups, with lower economic status, suffer as a result. For example, a poor woman from the low-status ethnic group called Mallah in Gajedi village remarked to the researcher with frustration that she and many other women from her ethnic group still spent a whole hour collecting water from the new tube-wells. Yet women from relatively well-off families spent hardly five to ten minutes in this task, because their male family-members had good contacts with the male project-staff and thus were able to influence the location of tube-wells, ensuring that they were installed close to their own homes. She observed that such discrepancy made her feel that women who were not benefiting equally from the improved water services should destroy the tube-wells, so that all women would then be on an equal footing in the community.

Because of their frequent contacts with the male project staff, the local men have achieved more access to and control over project resources, which has given them greater economic benefits, thus improving their status still further, and further widening the gap between the sexes. There were no attempts by the male project staff to improve women's knowledge, skills, self-esteem, and confidence.

The projects' over-reliance on men has deterred the local women from taking responsibility for the protection and management of water resources. As a result, the number of mal-functioning tube-wells is increasing in the project communities. Moreover, the local women are not showing any interest in becoming involved in other committee activities. A deeper analysis of the projects' impact shows that, despite the relatively easy access to improved water services, the local women have been able neither to meet their practical needs and concerns nor to improve their lives strategically.

Institutional bias

Further investigation of the causes of such an emphasis on men's participation over women's at the community level showed that all the policies and practices of the selected agencies are gender-biased. For example, there are more men participating in the policy-making bodies; the number of male staff is much higher than the number of female staff; the personnel policies (formulated by men, of course) do not encourage women to join or to continue working in the agencies; the institutional objectives and strategies do not emphasise the strategic needs and concerns of women. The project-management guidelines are not gender-aware; there are no funds available for addressing gender issues; and even in agencies where funds are not a problem, the male senior staff showed no real interest in allocating funds for gender and development (GAD) activities; despite all this, there is nobody particularly responsible for ensuring that gender-related concerns have been effectively addressed, either in the agencies or in the local communities; nor is there any provision to train the agency staff in gender-related aspects of development.

Challenges

The research findings show that addressing women's strategic issues and ensuring the sustainability of project benefits are inter-related. How can the agency technicians (mainly men) and local men and women working in the delivery of water supply be made aware of this relationship? An equally important question is how to help all these partners to understand the effects of a gender-insensitive project on existing gender relations in the project communities, and how a gender-sensitive project can benefit overall human well-being.

In order to improve the present situation, it is necessary to make the institutional policies and practices more gender-sensitive before addressing the gender issues at the community level. This is because what the male project staff do at the community level is guided by the agencies' policy documents, objectives and strategies, internal culture, and project-management guidelines. We recommend the following specific measures:

- organise gender training for all agency staff, and gender-sensitisation activities for community women and men;
- make provision for both human and capital resources, to ensure gender sensitivity in all agency work;
- increase the number of women in general at the agency level, and in paid and technical positions in particular at the community level;

- provide women with technical training that can yield income in the future, so as to improve their bargaining power, decision-making power, and status.

Moreover, since the research findings also show that the policies and practices of the agencies in the study have been heavily influenced by the international donors, who wield considerable financial power, there is also a need to make the water policies and practices of the donors more gender-sensitive. Finally, what is of the utmost importance is to make the education system, both in the schools and at higher levels, gender-aware through the provision of gender-sensitive textbooks and teaching methods, the appointment of gender-sensitive teachers, and the creation of a gender-sensitive environment. Also needed is an environment where girls get opportunities to go to school and continue their study up to higher levels together with their male counterparts.

Conclusion

We conclude that women's strategic involvement at the community level is possible only if the male project staff and their agencies are fully gender-aware. The challenge is how to make them truly gender-sensitive, so that they are not satisfied with women's tokenistic involvement.

As long as men do not assume their share of women's traditional tasks, over-burdened women cannot effectively participate in development projects; the challenge thus is how to motivate men to share women's traditional work. Men in general assume that water supply is a technical matter and that thus women have no influential roles to play in this sector; the challenge here is how to make the male technicians and the local men aware that water has not only a technical dimension but also social dimensions, and that thus women's strategic involvement is absolutely essential.

Tackling male exclusion in post-industrialised settings: lessons from the UK

Sue Smith

Gender inequality is preventing us from eliminating poverty. Gender equality should recognise both women's and men's needs, and how these interact. Usually women are at a disadvantage, but sometimes a special focus is needed on men and boys.
(*Breaking the Barrier*, Department for International Development Issues Paper, 1998)

Staff working on Oxfam's UK Poverty Programme responded with enthusiasm to an invitation to present a paper at the seminar on Men's Involvement in Gender and Development Policy and Practice, held in Oxford in June 2000. This was for three reasons. First, we wanted to set our practical experience of supporting community-based anti-poverty projects within conceptual frameworks provided by the seminar. Second, we wanted to promote an exchange of views between practitioners and academics: something that has proved to be a fruitful growing point for organisational learning in the past. Third, we felt that we needed the experience of reflecting on our work, in order to move forward our own thinking on the role of men in gender-equity initiatives.

Why men and why now?

For some time we have been aware that the changing nature of gender relations in British society requires us to take a fresh look at what is happening to men and women, and to make a start on modernising our own gender analysis. Changes in employment patterns, the nature of the family, and public attitudes to gender-related issues indicate many new developments in the social relations of women and men. However, we have also been aware of the dangers of concentrating on the experience of men, given Oxfam's remit to relieve poverty. These dangers are twofold. First, devoting time and resources to work with men seemed counter-productive, given entrenched gender-linked inequalities. Despite thirty years of legislation to ensure equal opportunities, women are still the majority in the poorest groups in British society. Secondly, there is the danger of reinforcing the backlash against women's claims to equality that has occurred in recent years. Despite improvements in women's position, it is still the case that the majority of senior decision makers and managers in the UK are men, and that the culture and structures of institutions are still formulated on the basis of men's social realities, which are perceived as the norm.

Faced with this dilemma, the Oxfam UK Poverty Programme decided to support a number of small projects involving disadvantaged men, to get a better picture of what was actually happening in their lives and the impact that social change was having on gender relations. This work has been small scale and experimental, but it could be significant for our gender and poverty analysis. This was what we wanted to present at the workshop.

Preparations for the workshop

We thought it important to spend some time talking to some of Oxfam's local partners, to get a better picture from their project workers of what was happening to men in marginalised communities. Several meetings were held. In the north of England we met with CREST and Withernsea Children and Family Action. In Scotland we reviewed a participatory appraisal carried out by East End Health Action and analysed what it was telling us about the different experiences of men and women.

Presentations

Programme Development Officers Julie Jarman (north of England) and Judith Robertson (Scotland) presented Oxfam-supported projects involving men in their regions, and drew out the common lessons.

- **Withernsea Children and Family Action** works on an isolated housing estate near Hull, in north-east England, with disadvantaged fathers and young men, concentrating on aspects of fatherhood and parenting. Oxfam has contributed to the cost of employing an outreach worker one day a week.

- St. George's Church and Family Centre set up a shop-front drop-in resource centre, **CREST**, on a housing estate in Salford, near Manchester. The centre provides a dedicated space where local men who have been unemployed for long periods of time can develop their skills and confidence, and make use of advice and drop-in facilities. Oxfam has contributed to the start-up costs.

- **East End Health Action**, a small community health project in Glasgow, ran a series of workshops, using participatory appraisal (PA) methods that included getting men and women to map their experience in single-sex groups. The workshop revealed the differing attitudes of young women and men to issues such as territoriality, drug addiction, and parenting, which could be significant in formulating health-policy priorities. Oxfam supported the costs of a consultant to train EEHA workers in PA methods.

Common issues

Men's and women's attitudes

- Men feel that they lack clarity about their roles, especially since the widespread disappearance of full-time jobs, with which they still identify. They feel confused about where they fit into their families and into paid or community work in what now seems to them to be a woman's world.

- It is harder for project workers to reach and engage with men, as they are more defensive than women and put up more barriers; more effort is need to gain their trust. Women's attitude to opportunity offered is: *What can I get out of this?*, whereas men's attitude is: *What's the catch?*

- Men seem not to be 'join-ers': they are fearful of getting involved in a group and they do not in general function well in them.

- Young men and women have very different perceptions of the nature of problems that affect them, and the possible solutions. For example, the territorial barriers imposed by gangs are very real for boys, but not a problem for girls. In relation to parenting, boys concentrate on their role as providers,

whereas girls have a more holistic and socialised view of their parental responsibilities.

What kinds of project succeed?

- Both sets of Project workers agreed that advertising initiatives as 'men's projects' can be counter-productive. A more successful strategy is to attract men by offering recreational activities such as fishing and gardening, or to offer training in technical skills such as photography and information technology.

- Fatherhood and the family are a key entry-point when working with men, because these things concern what they are and what they do.

- CREST's experience is that men are put under more pressure than women to get work, especially by government-run Job Centres. The turnover of men using CREST appears to be higher than the turnover of women using an equivalent centre.

- Younger men are willing to undergo training, but the self-image of older men is closely connected to the idea of being in paid employment, and they seem fearful of involvement in education.

- Withernsea staff reported that when they visited women's centres to gather information and learn from their expertise, a number were actively hostile towards them and their work.

What kinds of project worker operate best with groups of men?

- Staff of both CREST and the Withernsea project were agreed that the best results are achieved with male project workers who have 'street credibility' and are recruited locally and known to men in the community.

- It is hard to find male project workers with appropriate skills, and recruitment is equally difficult. This may be because men perceive 'caring' work as being a female profession, and therefore as having a low status.

- The most common pattern is still for women to enter voluntary work through community self-help initiatives, whereas for men the entry point is higher: they tend to go straight into community management work at a professional level.

Discussion: how and where to work with men?

Following the presentations at the seminar, discussion focused on the barriers to working with men in the UK. The barriers exist at a number of levels. Practitioners disagree both about the need for a focus on men, and about how to work with them. A number of questions were explored. Are we engaged in a mirror-image of the debates about how to address women's empowerment? What methods should we be using to explore the changing relationship between gender and poverty? Should men's disadvantage, if it exists, be tackled in separate or mixed groups? What are the dangers of 'adding men in', in the way that women used to be added in to development programmes? Should there be separate groups for men to work on some issues, and if so, which ones?

Even if there was acceptance that working with men was an important means to achieve gender equity, participants at the seminar could not offer clear and workable strategies. Some echoed the experience of Oxfam's partners, asserting that it is hard to reach and engage with men at all. Men do not come forward readily to join men's groups. Men's groups are few in number, and fragile in nature. Community groups tend to be run by women. Women rather than men tend to occupy leadership positions at community level, although they find it hard to make the transition into being decision makers in larger bodies and at higher levels. Can it be argued that the conditions that prevailed in the early days of Women and Development are now being replicated in reverse, so that now it is men who need to be heard, and brought into community development at the grassroots level?

The effects of these barriers are compounded by the gender-blind policies of funders and decision-makers – a fact that was emphasised by the experience of East End Health Action, and corroborated by other participants. EEHA's participatory appraisal took place in a gender-blind policy vacuum. Neither the local authority that commissioned the work, nor the Social Inclusion Partnership in which it was framed, was aware that men's and women's perceptions and needs might be different, that different outcomes might be appropriate for men or women, or even that a choice might be necessary. The workshops revealed that gang culture and territoriality was a big issue for boys, but not for girls, yet solutions to the problems of territoriality were reported as the key issue. This is echoed at a national level, where lack of 'joined-up' government thinking would bring together the work of the Women's Unit and the Social Exclusion Unit and other departments in a holistic and gender-sensitive approach to policy making.

Outcomes

For the UK Poverty Programme the seminar represented a step forward. It has stimulated interest among colleagues in Oxfam, and placed our practical experience on the table for analysis. The next steps for us were to commission a survey of projects and research that apply a poverty and equity focus to community-development work with men, in various regions of the UK. We expect to disseminate the results of this piece of work in 2001.

Challenging *machismo* to promote sexual and reproductive health: working with Nicaraguan men

Peter Sternberg

Men's participation in the promotion of sexual health is seen by many as a promising strategy (Drennon 1998). However, apart from very few recent interventions such as Stepping Stones, an HIV-prevention programme based on gender relationships (Welbourn 1995), and Fathers Inc., a Jamaican peer-based approach to promoting adolescent men's sexual health (Lize 1998), health-promotion programmes have been slow to take up the challenge.

In 1996, the Centro de Información y Servicios de Asesoría en Salud (CISAS), a prominent Nicaraguan health-promotion NGO, began working with groups of men, mainly in response to demands by women from some of the poor communities where it works. The women argued that it is all very well working with women and girls to promote sexual and reproductive health and empowerment, but if you really want things to change, you have to work with men too.

From its inception in 1983, CISAS has worked from a perspective of community empowerment, with a particular emphasis on empowering women. However, CISAS has recognised that the health-promotion agenda of many organisations is conservative and male-oriented, generally viewing women as vehicles for reproduction or the transmission of illness, rather than as valued individuals (Wilton 1994). This stance not only ignores women's needs as individuals (Doyal 1991), but also ignores men as a group (Barker 1996). As a result, such approaches reiterate women's responsibility for health, especially for reproductive health, while ignoring the possibility that men could play a positive and proactive role alongside women in promoting their own health and the health of their families and communities (Wegner et al. 1998).

There is a conventional assumption that men are sexually voracious, careless, and irresponsible. Men who conform to this stereotype are unlikely to be much concerned about the possibilities of fathering an unplanned child or contracting HIV or other sexually transmitted diseases. However, the image is not borne out by reality. For example, citing his own research carried out in Puerto Rico in the 1950s, Stycos, the veteran health promoter and family planner, stresses that the men whom he interviewed were far from 'the sex-crazed males anxious to demonstrate their fertility' (Stycos 1996: 2) that he had been led to expect. What he found instead was that expectations and norms of male and female behaviour made communication between men and women, especially on matters concerning sex and sexuality, very difficult. Stycos identified this lack of communication between the sexes as an important aspect governing sexual behaviour, and concluded that there was a need to work with men in highlighting the benefits of family planning to them as individuals. It is only by establishing a men's agenda in matters of reproductive health that things will change: a lesson, Stycos says, which has too often been ignored, and one that CISAS is taking seriously.

CISAS hoped, through its research, to provide men with a body of information that they could use to understand their behaviour, attitudes, and the context of these, in order to develop an awareness of the social and cultural norms defined by *machismo*, and the way in which these norms create a certain model of 'acceptable' male sexual behaviour, and a particular set of attitudes. Individual men needed to consider the degree of similarity between their actual behaviour and attitudes and the stereotypical model of masculinity with which they are presented, the model that in Nicaragua constitutes the *machismo* system. Second, CISAS aimed to encourage men to consider the effect of their behaviour on themselves and on other people. It was hoped that, by helping men to think through these issues, it would be possible to change the power relationships that lead individual men to put themselves and others at risk.

The Nicaraguan context

Following the revolution in Nicaragua in 1979,[1] one of the aims of the Sandinista government was to foster more stable and egalitarian families, and to enshrine equal rights for women within the constitution (Lancaster 1992). In this aim, as in so many others, the Sandinistas failed, owing to a combination of war, bad planning, and economic instability which culminated, in 1990, in their electoral defeat.

The two governments that followed have pursued neo-liberal monetarist policies, and adopted structural adjustment programmes set up by the World Bank (Vargas 1998). Over the past ten years, these policies have caused not only rising prices and stagnating wages, but also a rise in unemployment and a rapid expansion of the 'informal economy'. The gap between the 'haves' and the 'have nots' has widened dramatically: today, more than 70 per cent of the population live below the poverty line (ibid.). Managua, once one of the safest cities in Latin America, has become a battle-ground for rival gangs of young men; violent crime, robbery, prostitution, and sexual tourism are on the increase (CENIDH 1998). The country and the economy have also been afflicted by a series of natural disasters, culminating with Hurricane Mitch in 1998. Some 865,700 people were directly affected by the hurricane, losing their homes, their livelihoods, or both (Alforja 1999).

One result of this instability has been the exponential growth of Nicaragua's civil society since 1990, in an attempt to fill the gaps left by government inaction and indifference. CISAS and other Nicaraguan NGOs have been in the forefront of championing human rights, and have managed to keep gender-linked power relations more or less on the policy agenda. Nicaraguan NGOs have had some notable successes, including the passing of a law that made intrafamilial violence a crime punishable by imprisonment, and the establishment of several pilot projects of a new police service staffed by officers specially trained to deal with crimes against women and children. Despite these initiatives, police reported that in 1998 crimes against women and children had increased by 17 per cent from their 1997 levels (INEC 1999).

Nicaraguan women continue to be under-represented in the public sphere and abused in their private lives (Montenegro 1997). Only 11 per cent of National Assembly legislators and 25 per cent of the Nicaraguan members of the Central American Parliament are women (CENIDH 1998). The official 1998 demographic and health survey, ENDESA-98 (INEC 1999), suggested that 29 per cent of Nicaraguan women have been physically or sexually abused by their male partners. Of these, more than 46 per cent had been abused in the previous 12 months (ibid.). The Nicaraguan media are conservative in their representation of women (Montenegro 1997), a fact brought home to many Nicaraguans by their virtual silence on the continuing refusal of former Sandinista president Daniel Ortega to recant his senatorial immunity in order to answer charges of sexual abuse brought by his stepdaughter in 1998.[2]

Health and sexuality in Nicaragua

Statistics about sexual and reproductive health in Nicaragua reveal that, although almost all of the women (over 95 per cent) who took part in the 1998 national demographic survey had heard of modern contraceptive methods, only 60 per cent of women of fertile age were users in 1998 (INEC 1999). Some 15 per cent of women consider their contraceptive needs unmet (ibid.). Although contraception is legally available, government policy emphasises the need for sexual morality and abstinence until marriage (GHCV 1997). Sex education in schools is taught within a framework of 'family values', which views sex as a necessary evil for perpetuating the species (ibid.). This may be one of the reasons why the Nicaraguan fertility rate is one of the highest in Latin America, at an average of 3.9 children per woman of fertile age (INEC 1999). It may also help to explain why, by the age of 19, 46 per cent of women have been pregnant at some time (ibid.). In Nicaragua, abortion is illegal except for medical reasons, and even then, abortions can be legally performed only with the permission of three doctors, and the woman's partner or guardian. Unsurprisingly, there is a high rate of illegal abortions, many performed under unsafe conditions (Pizarro 1996).

In 1998, the Ministry of Health recorded an incidence of 153 cases of sexually transmitted diseases (STDs) per 100,000 people. By September 1999, some 476 cases of HIV infection had been reported since 1987, in a population of 4.8m people. The Ministry of

Health recognises that there is substantial under-reporting of STDs, including HIV, and the actual figures are probably much higher (MINSA 1999). The organisation that co-ordinates HIV-prevention initiatives for Central America argues that, although reported numbers of infections are low, the population is at risk because of its young demographic profile, high fertility rate, and low or irregular usage of condoms (PASCA 1997).

Machismo and the Nicaraguan man

Almost without exception, studies of gender and sexuality in Nicaragua highlight one over-arching aspect of the culture: *machismo*. There is no English word which adequately translates this term, but *machismo* could be described as a cult of the male: a heady mixture of paternalism, aggression, systematic subordination of women, fetishism of their bodies, and idolisation of their reproductive and nurturing capacities, coupled with a rejection of homosexuality. The Central American psychologist, Martín Baró (1988), characterises it as a strong tendency towards, and valuing of, genital activity (that is, penetration); a frequent tendency towards bodily aggression; a carefully cultivated devil-may-care attitude or indifference towards any activity which does not clearly reinforce masculinity; and *Guadalupismo*, a hypersensitivity towards the idealised notion of women as virgins or mothers.

Machismo is present not only in the behaviour of individual men: it is manifested in political and social institutions and deeply ingrained in the culture (Monzón 1988). *Machismo* has been seen as a system of political organisation — 'a political economy of the body' (Lancaster 1992: 236) — in which the cult of the male is an important underpinning of the productive and reproductive economy. *Machismo* gives rise to powerful images that legitimate women's subordination and establish a value system which is concerned with regulating relationships — not so much between men and women, but relationships between men, in which women are conceived of as a form of currency.

A serious problem with using *machismo* to explain men's behaviour is that prevailing values are constantly being redefined. This state of flux seems to be an integral part of Nicaraguan society: as the political commentator and sociologist, Oscar Rene Vargas, points out: 'As a country, Nicaragua is eternally searching for an identity and oscillating, in an ambivalent way, between old and modern, tradition and fashion, native and foreign' (Vargas 1999: 19; my translation). This oscillation belies any attempt to explain Nicaraguan culture, or the political and social system, in terms of single-word concepts like *machismo*, or for that matter 'neoliberal', 'conservative', or 'catholic'. Such labels cannot be used, either, to explain or predict men's behaviour. However, helping Nicaraguan men to understand themselves, and the way in which *machismo* operates in their lives, might provide men with reasons to participate in actions aimed at altering the oppressive structures which maintain women's subordination and exploitation.

The study

Our research examined men's knowledge, attitudes, and behaviour in three areas fundamental to the social construction of masculinity: sexuality, reproduction, and fatherhood. It aimed to provide information which could be used for planning further work with men, to help them to develop an understanding of their role in the promotion of sexual and reproductive health. The study formed the first part of a pilot project to involve men in health promotion in their communities.

In all, 90 men were recruited for inclusion in the study, from five urban and three rural communities in various parts of Nicaragua where CISAS was already working with groups of women and children. They were aged from 15 to 70. Seventy per cent were married and/or living with their partners; 30 per cent were single. The average number of children fathered by each man was 4.7. Forty per cent of participants had been educated to primary level or less, 50 per cent had secondary education, and 10 per cent had tertiary education.

Work began with a workshop in August 1997. CISAS health educators invited 38 men from the communities mentioned above who had previously participated in CISAS activities (such as community meetings and discussion groups). During the workshop, participants discussed issues related to sexuality, fatherhood, and reproduction with health educators, in small groups and in plenaries. Participants also completed a biographical questionnaire which included questions about their values and practical experience of contraception and fatherhood.

Using the questionnaire results, a small team of CISAS staff put together a guide for in-depth interviews and focus-group discussions on the same key issues as the initial workshop. Participants for these were men from the CISAS target communities who had not participated in the workshop. Ten men were interviewed, two from each of the five regions where CISAS works; and five focus-group meetings (one in each region) were held with eight men in each group. CISAS health educators recruited men who had participated from time to time in CISAS activities such as discussion groups or community meetings.

Many men seem to find it liberating to discuss close relationships and sexuality with other men. After the workshop, and after almost every interview and focus-group discussion, participants came up to researchers to thank them for the opportunity to share their opinions with other men about these rather intimate subjects. Many commented that it was the first time in their lives they had had this opportunity.

In qualitative research, not only the content but also the context of what is said is important (Miller and Glasner 1997). In any verbal interaction, speakers assume that what is said will produce a particular reaction in the interlocutor (Potter 1997); if the reaction is not the desired one, the speaker will change or correct what he or she says. While some regard this as problematic for researchers, because it implies that sociological research is always subject to contextual bias, others argue that it is very useful, since it shows how established norms influence people's behaviour (May 1993). In our research, participants contradicted themselves, or clarified their comments, when they were afraid that what they had said might cast aspersions on their masculinity, or on the image that they wanted to project as reasonable, rational, and caring people. These two inter-related sets of values underlie what was said and informed the relationships between participants, and between participants and facilitators. The comments and opinions reported below must be seen in this context.

Some results

Attitudes to sexuality

An important theme in the discussions about sexuality was the belief that male sexuality is governed by instinct, and that it is something 'wild' which men need to make an effort to control. In all focus groups, men expressed pride in their stereotypical image as sexually voracious conquerors of women and therefore 'real men'. Such comments indicate that the first thing that every man does on meeting a woman is to evaluate her as a possible sexual conquest. According to participants, such an evaluation involves primarily her *parametros físicos* (physical appearance) and, secondly, her marital status: '*Men, because they want to be machos, say that "whatever goes into the broiler is meat"... I've had sex with cousins, not with aunts, you understand, you have to respect them a bit more.*'

In focus groups, all participants spoke of their sexuality in terms of force and strength, and of female sexuality in terms of beauty and passivity. Participants stated that 'honest' women should not have opinions on what they want in sex: it is up to the man to know how to please them. While many participants pointed out that sexuality had much to do with how people communicate, none of the participants identified communication as something that they felt they had, or that they desired, with their partners.

Focus-group participants were asked about the qualities of the ideal female partner. The consensus was that she has a beautiful body, but more importantly that she is a cook and household manager, who is willing and able to serve her man faithfully and be a good mother to his children. The ideal male was seen as a worker who earns enough money to support his wife and children: his role is to provide financially for his family's needs. He does not drink, take drugs, or womanise. Despite this, 26 per cent of the men who attended the workshop reported having more than one partner 'at the moment'. In discussions in the focus groups, it became evident that having more than one partner is seen not just as a man's right, but also as an important expression of his sexuality: '*From the moment I meet a woman that I fancy, I'm thinking that I'll do something with her, I'm going to get to know her and have an adventure; I can't stop it, it's part of me*'; and '*We're unfaithful by nature, I guess men are just born bad.*'

In comparison, a woman's infidelity is considered to be a different thing altogether: women, unlike men, are not by nature unfaithful. Unfaithful women are therefore 'bad' women. This is a good example of the double morality that is a salient feature of Nicaraguan *machismo*. However, a woman's infidelity is a reflection not only of her wickedness but also of her husband's failure, because apparently he cannot satisfy her sexually.

Men showed varying degrees of homophobia. To many in the study, homosexuality is 'against nature' and against 'God's will'. Homosexuality was regarded as an illness with a direct physical cause, such as a 'brain tumour' or a 'small penis'. Some believed that it could be caught, as though it was a sexually transmitted disease. Others saw homosexuality as a result of society's loss of values. During discussions on this topic in the workshop, several men pointed out that society's views condemning homosexuality had a direct impact on the way in which they relate to other men. There are certain things that men cannot do without being singled out as *cochones* (a derogatory term for homosexual men). These were not, as might be expected, tasks seen as women's work: they relate, instead, to how men relate to each other. For example, a man cannot comment on the beauty of another man: '*I don't want to say in public or in private, "this guy is handsome, beautiful, pretty", because they'll mark me down as a queer.*'

Discussions about lesbianism highlighted the fact that men's sexuality is centred on the penis and penetration, since many could not conceive of a sexual relationship without penetration. The participants of two groups took this to extraordinary lengths, believing with unshakeable confidence that lesbians have penises (albeit somewhat smaller ones than men: '*2 to 3 inches*'). Focus-group participants spent much time trying to identify a direct cause for lesbianism. Most felt that it was due to the failure of men to please women sexually, but this was generally seen as the woman's fault: she must be the kind of woman that men cannot please.

Attitudes to reproduction

Men expressed the opinion that within a marriage or a stable relationship, it is a man's right to decide when a woman should have children. This was never stated directly, but it was implicit in many of the comments about contraception. Participants felt this was because they were the ones who would be expected to provide for the children. Eighty-seven per cent of workshop participants, and every focus group, were in favour of contraception. It was clear from focus-group and interview information that the main reason for participants' support of contraception was because it prevented them from having to take economic responsibility for unwanted children. As one man pointed out: '*For me, family planning is important. I wouldn't want to have any more because of my condition. I'm poor and wouldn't like any more children.*'

Despite this, using contraception is still seen as a sin, as could be seen clearly in comments from the 13 per cent of workshop participants who expressed opinions against it: '*It's a sin. You see, only God knows what a child's destiny is. If God wants a child, he makes one, it is a sin to prevent it.*' Many participants referred to it as sinful even while justifying its use, as in this comment by a workshop participant: '*It's a sin, but, for me, it's more sinful to bring a mountain of children into the world and not know what to do with them; having them crying of hunger and not being able to feed them. That's a bigger sin.*'

Statistics about the number of men in Nicaragua who abandon their pregnant partners are not available, but the percentage of female-headed households is very high, at 31 per cent of all households (INEC 1999). Almost exclusively, men in the study saw financial problems as the reason for abandoning partners and children. However, many did say they felt strongly that it was 'unmanly' to run away from the responsibility: '*As a man, you have to take the responsibility, whether it's your wife or your lover or whatever, you can't reject it. Even if you have two women, you have to hide it from the woman you live with. Denying the responsibility wouldn't be manly.*'

Despite such views, the consensus from interviews and focus groups was that using contraception is not men's responsibility. Among focus-group participants, knowledge of how the different methods worked was poor, even among men with higher levels of education. Most discussions centred on the condom, vasectomy, and female sterilisation, probably because these were seen to be the most controversial methods.

Publicity by CISAS and other organisations about condom use had clearly been received by men in the study. Several repeated the slogans from the publicity proudly, and without prompting, during the workshop. However, while men in the study knew that condoms could prevent HIV infection and unwanted pregnancy, there was general agreement that very few men use them. Different reasons were cited for this, including illiteracy, the fact that the woman was known to be an 'honest woman', and the fact that sex with condoms does not feel the same. Despite this, some 68 per cent of workshop participants reported that they had used condoms within the past six months. It became clear that men felt that the only women they needed to use condoms with were those whom they judged to be 'suspicious': women in bars, and women whose pasts they did not know. One interviewee summed up the majority view: *'When you see a very suspicious woman you might use it, but sometimes when you meet a woman, maybe who's engaged, but allows you to do it, there's no need to use a preservative. You know, they just don't feel the same, it's like attaching a hose or something, you just don't feel right.'*

Vasectomy was said to affect the character of the man, making him 'like a woman'. This view expressed a fear that many seemed to feel: that losing their ability to father children would affect their manhood. Having said this, not all men were opposed to vasectomy; a few said that they would have the operation, because it was a safe and sure method of contraception which would prevent them from having to take economic responsibility for more children. Only one man admitted that he had actually had the operation.

Female sterilisation, more than any other contraceptive method, made men suspect that their partners wanted to have sex with other men. In the questionnaire, participants' responses to questions about female sterilisation reveal widespread fear of women's infidelity. Twenty-nine per cent of respondents to the questionnaire agreed with the statement: *'After women have the operation, they look for other men to have sex with.'* In discussions, even men who said that they were not against female sterilisation first alluded to, and then dismissed, the infidelity myth: *'If she wants to get sterilised it's because she's crazy, she wants to cheat on her husband, she wants to have one man and then another.'*

Attitudes to abortion

More than 92 per cent of the men in the workshop regarded abortion as a sin. In the focus groups, women who have abortions were termed 'murderers'. Men were asked in the groups and interviews why they thought abortions happened. They cited medical reasons, but also understood that many abortions take place for social reasons, which include relationship and economic problems. In focus groups, the consensus was that abortions were the fault of irresponsible women, highlighting the fact that most men do not see contraception as their responsibility.

The situation is slightly different for young, unmarried women. Men do not expect them to be responsible or to be able to resist seduction. Unwanted pregnancies in unmarried young women were seen as resulting from loss of parental control, and especially of fathers' control. However, even for young women, men saw the solution as having the child and giving it away.

Attitudes to fatherhood

All men in the study who had children talked of feeling mature after the birth of their first children, as though fatherhood provides a man with an entrance into 'real' adulthood. For most, these feelings went hand-in-hand with the realisation that they were now responsible for the child's upbringing. One man explained that, after the birth of a child, men feel a mixture of joy and worry over how they will be able to cope financially with the extra burden: *'In the moment [when your child is just born] you feel great, but then, well, you know, you start thinking, you're broke, and it's also worrying.'*

According to participants in four focus groups, providing economically for children is a father's principal role. The other main paternal responsibility is teaching children how to behave. Men felt that this is done through teaching children important values, including the value of work, honesty, responsibility, and respect for one's elders. These two responsibilities, as provider and disciplinarian, were the only two mentioned; only one man spoke of 'giving love' as a paternal responsibility. On the other hand, it was very obvious that most men in the study value the love of their children, and the time that they spend with them. In the questionnaire, over 95 per cent remarked that playing with their children was important to them. In groups and interviews, many men talked with pride of their children's affection for them.

Most men in the study reported that they involved themselves 'from time to time' in practical child-care. Activities mentioned included feeding, bathing, dressing, and even washing and ironing clothes. However, day-to-day child-care was seen as a help and support for mothers, rather than as part of a father's role.

The men were asked about the content of the last conversation that they had had with their children. Almost all the men said that they had been giving advice; only one man reported a discussion about a topic which did not have to do with control or discipline. It would seem from this that fathers either lack skills to communicate with their children in other ways, or do not see the importance of this. Many said they find it particularly difficult to communicate with their daughters, and that they are often stricter with them than with their sons. The reason cited for this was that fathers need to be especially vigilant with their daughters, to prevent them from becoming pregnant. Relationships between fathers and their daughters were generally seen as more difficult. One possible reason for this may be that daughters are regarded as less valuable than sons. A daughter is not valueless, but it appears that her value lies in her ability to serve her family, and not in her as a human being. As one man said: '*When I realised that God had given me a girl, I said to myself, "at least I have a cook to make me tortillas".*'

Insights from the research

In many studies, *machismo* and the ideas on which it is based tend to act as an explanation (and, occasionally, an excuse) for men's behaviour. However, using *machismo* as an explanation or excuse assumes that the concept shapes men's conduct. In fact, perhaps its main effect is to present Nicaraguan society with a conventional model of men's and women's behaviour, which individuals may or may not adhere to. The results of this research should not be seen as a picture of a single, objective Nicaraguan *machismo* operating in interpersonal relationships, but as a snapshot of complicated, endlessly changing relationships between participants, their partners, and their children, and between participants and researchers.

If the research has little predictive value for men's behaviour in the context of their relationships, because it cannot depict the context, or explain the behaviour of individual men in their relationships with women and children, why spend good money in a poor country to do it?

Challenging male hegemony

It is necessary, as well as morally defensible, to use development methods which are based on a commitment to empowerment and active participation. Norms of masculinity are so artificial, and so inhuman, that they need to be policed to maintain them (Formaini 1990). Institutions which do this policing include the church, the government, the media, the medical profession, and — most effectively — the family (Schifter and Madrigal 1996). Together, these institutions put into place a system of discipline that affects the social behaviour of individual men and women under male leadership or rule (Connell 1995). As feminists have contended, empowered individuals not only can challenge male hegemony and norms of gender relations, but also play a significant role in reformulating these relations, which would result in true emancipation (Holland and Ramazanoglu 1994).

Participatory methods based on a commitment to empowerment have rarely been applied to work which focuses on men as gendered beings. Much has been written on the need to focus on women's participation through the use of women-only groups, as well as by facilitating their full involvement in mixed groups, but the suggestion that a powerful group such as men may require specific attention is new and challenging.

Persuading men to participate in health promotion

Agencies which are reluctant to work with men on issues concerning sexual and reproductive health (Stycos 1996) may justify this policy by saying that men have little or no interest in the theme. However, CISAS's experience is that men are very interested — once they can be persuaded to take part. One reason for men's unwillingness to be recruited as participants in such projects as ours may be their perception that health promotion is women's work. Possibly, development agencies themselves have had a major influence in this perception, since few efforts have been made to involve men in proactive community development programmes. Many men, and some development agencies, continue to view men's participation as unnecessary, and even counter-productive (Drennon 1998).

For some women, the proposition that men might be involved in initiatives to promote sexual health seems threatening. As Marge

Berer (1996) points out, many women are suspicious of health planners' aim to increase men's participation in the promotion of reproductive and sexual health, viewing this as part of a campaign which aims to win back power for men. It is possible that these fears are well grounded, as they are founded on the bitter experience of the 1960s sexual revolution which, for all its rhetoric of sexual freedom, did little to change the subordinate role that women play in most sexual relations with men (Hawkes 1996). This is supported by some evidence that men's involvement in family planning has actually increased their control over the fertility of women, rather than resulted in women having more choice (Cornwall 1998). There is also a danger that efforts to persuade men to participate will take away funds from projects that target women and children, and will ultimately result in re-establishing a male-dominated and male-orientated agenda (Berer 1996; Helzner 1996).

These warnings should not go unheeded. The setting and application of a men's agenda for sexual-health promotion should not result in the curtailment of services for women because funds are being reallocated to men (AVSC International 1997), nor should it give men the keys to more subtle forms of domination and exploitation. Ultimately, as feminists have long realised, men's participation in the reformation of gender relationships is a two-edged sword. Kimmel and Mesner (1995) point out that, by making the processes of patriarchy visible to men, there is a risk that they will learn new ways of maintaining or even increasing its power, rather than reforming the norms upon which it is based. The job of ensuring that this does not occur lies fairly, if not squarely, in the hands of professional health promoters working with men.

Notes

1   For a useful introduction to Nicaraguan social and political history up to 1990, see K. Norsworthy (1990) *Nicaragua: A country guide*, The Interhemispheric Education Resource Centre, Albuquerque, New Mexico.

2   For an interesting review (in Spanish) of the way in which the patriarchy handled the case, see J. R. Huerta (1998) *El Silencio del Patriarcha*, Managua: Renacimiento.

References

Alforja, A. (1999) 'Propuesta ante la Reunión de Estocolmo para la reconstrucción y transformación de Nicaragua', Managua: Coordinadora Civil para la Emergencia y la Recontracción (CCER).

AVSC International (1998) 'Men as Partners Initiative: Summary report of literature review and case studies', New York: AVSC International.

Barker, G. (1996) 'The Misunderstood Gender: Male Involvement in the Family and in Reproductive and Sexual Health in Latin America and the Caribbean', Chicago: John D and Catherine T Macarthur Foundation.

Baró, M. (1988) *Acción e Ideología. Psicología Social de Centroamérica*, University of Central America (UCA), San Salvador, El Salvador.

Berer, M. (1996) 'Men', *Reproductive Health Matters*, 7 May 1996.

CENIDH (1998) 'Derechos Humanos en Nicaragua', Centro Nicaragüense de Derechos Humanos, Managua.

Connell, R. (1995) *Masculinities*, Oxford: Polity Press/Blackwell.

Cornwall, A. (1998) 'Beyond reproduction: Changing perspectives on gender and health', *Bridge*, 7, http://www.ids.ac.uk/ids/research/bridge (accessed 31 January 1999).

Doyal, L. (1991) 'Promoting women's health', in B. Badura and I. Kickbusch (eds) *Health Promotion Research*, Copenhagen: WHO.

Drennon, M. (1998) 'Reproductive Health: New Perspectives on Men's Participation', Population Reports, Johns Hopkins University School of Public Health, Population Information Program.

Formaini, C. (1990) *Men: The Darker Continent*, London: Heinemann.

GHCV (1997) *Responsibilidad Masculina en Salud Sexual y Reproductiva*, Grupo de Hombres Contra la Violencia, Managua: RSMLAC, SI Mujer.

Hawkes, G. (1996) *A Sociology of Sex and Sexuality*, Buckingham, England: Open University.

Helzner, J. (1996) 'Men's involvement in family planning', *Reproductive Health Matters*, 7, 146–54, May.

Holland, J. and C. Ramazanoglu (1994) 'Coming to conclusions: power and interpretation: researching young women's sexuality', in M. Maynard and J. Purvis (eds) *Researching Women's Lives from a Feminist Perspective*, London: Taylor and Walker.

INEC (1999) *'Encuesta Nicaragüense de Demografía y Salud – 1998'*, Managua: Instituto Nacional de Estadístícas y Censos (INEC).

Kimmel, M. and M. Mesner (1995) 'Introduction' in Kimmel and Mesner (eds) *Men's Lives* (3rd edition), Needham Heights, Mass.: Allyn and Bacon.

Lancaster, R. (1992) *Life is Hard: Machismo, Danger, and the Intimacy of Power in Nicaragua*, University of California, Berkeley.

Lize, S. (1998) 'Masculinity and men's health needs: a Jamaican perspective', *Bridge*, 7, http://www.ids.ac.uk/ids/research/bridge (accessed 31 January 1999).

May, T. (1993) *Social Research: Issues, Methods and Process*, Buckingham, England: Open University Press.

Miller J. and B. Glasner (1997) 'The "inside" and the "outside": finding realities in interviews', in D. Silverman (ed) (1997).

MINSA (1999) 'Plan Estratégico Nacional de Lucha Contra ETS/VIH/SIDA: Nicaragua 2000 – 2004', Managua: Ministry of Health of the Republic of Nicaragua.

Montenegro, S. (1997) *La revolución simbólica pendiente: mujeres, medios de comunicación y política*, CINCO, Managua.

Monzón A. (1988) 'El machismo: mito de la supremacia masculina', *Nueva Sociedad*, 93 (Jan-Feb), pp 148-62.

PASCA (1997) 'Resumen de País – la Situación del VIH/SIDA en Nicaragua', Managua: Proyecto Acción SIDA de Centro América (PASCA).

Pizarro, A. (1996) 'A Tu Salud', Managua: SI Mujer.

Potter, J. (1997) 'Discourse analysis as a way of analysing naturally occurring talk' in D. Silverman (ed) (1997).

Schifter, J. and J. Madrigal (1996) 'Las Gavetas Sexuales del Costarricense y el Riesgo de Infeccion con el VIH', San Jose, Costa Rica: Editorial IMEDIEX.

Silverman, D. (ed) (1997) *Qualitative Research: Theory, Method and Practice*, London: Sage.

Stycos, M. (1996) 'Men, Couples and Family Planning: A retrospective look', Working Paper No 96,12, Cornell University Population and Development Program, Cornell University.

Vargas, O-R (1998) 'Pobreza en Nicaragua: un abismo que se agranda', Managua: Centro de Estudios de la Realidad Nacional (CEREN).

Vargas, O-R (1999) 'El Síndrome de Pedrarias', Managua: Centro de Estudios de la Realidad Nacional (CEREN).

Wegner, M, E. Landry, D. Wilkinson, and J. Tzanis (1998) 'Men as partners in reproductive health: from issues to action', *International Family Planning Perspective*, 24:1, 38–42.

Welbourn, A. (1995) 'Stepping Stones: A training package on HIV/AIDS, communication and relationship skills', London: ActionAid.

Wilton, T. (1994) 'Feminism and the erotics of health promotion', in L, Doyal, J. Naidoo, and T. Wilton (eds) *Women and AIDS: Setting a Feminist Agenda*, London: Taylor and Francis.

Men and child-welfare services in the UK

Sandy Ruxton

Men rarely come into contact with child-welfare services in the UK, either as workers or users. This appears to hold true across a range of settings, including child-health clinics, family-planning centres, antenatal classes, day-care facilities, and family centres.

A central feature of all of these child-welfare institutions is of course that they are 'gendered'. Although there have been many laudable attempts to alter the balance, in practice the workers and users are almost always women, and service provision and policy design continue to draw heavily on the enduring ideological assumption — present also within wider society — that child-care is 'women's work'. Conversely, men are still seen first and foremost as breadwinners. This perspective remains largely intact, despite the fact that men's roles inside and outside the family — and women's roles to a much greater extent — have shifted significantly over the past thirty years, as a result of accelerating economic and social change.

This dominant and narrow approach to gender roles in the UK has a long pedigree. Since the Second World War, there has been widespread acceptance of the 'maternal deprivation' thesis promoted by writers such as Bowlby and Winnicott: if women remain the primary carers, it is because biology dictates that they should be. But although academic research, largely from a feminist perspective, has significantly undermined this case since the 1970s, it is still lodged in public consciousness and debate.

Rather than accept this defeatist biological line, a more convincing explanation of men's limited involvement in child-rearing is provided by Chodorow's psychoanalytical work.[1] She suggests that because women are usually the main carers for children, the first emotional ties that boys and girls form are to women. As they grow up, boys then face substantial pressure to deny this early feminine attachment in order to feel properly masculine, and this conditioning lasts into adulthood. In line with this theory, few men work in or attend child-welfare services, because they believe these environments to be 'non-masculine', and most men — in particular most heterosexual men — do not want to be so considered.

Sociological approaches are useful in highlighting the social/structural reasons why child-care is defined as 'women's work'; such factors include its low status, lack of power, and poor pay. Encouraging men to play a greater role in caring for children is an important step towards shifting this definition. Although there are some risks, enabling men to demonstrate their capacity to care is a challenge which is integral to the promotion of gender equality, and which will also have significant benefits for children's development.

There is now a significant body of research, both in the UK and internationally, which shows that men can participate fully in child-rearing, and that in terms of positive outcomes it makes little difference whether it is the mother or father who is the primary carer.[2] In practice, although mothers continue to carry the major share of household and child-care responsibilities, the National Child Development Study, which has tracked a UK birth cohort since 1958, shows that parents in dual-earner households commonly report that child-care is equally shared. Moreover, in 36 per cent of households with children, fathers are the main carers while mothers are out at work.[3]

The extent of the increase in male involvement within the home in child-care (and other domestic tasks) should not be overstated, but even this limited evidence provides some grounds for believing that a cultural shift is underway, incremental and long-term though it may be. If one accepts that this is happening, it is essential to understand how policy and practice can best encourage and support men (as well as women) in caring for children.

How can services support men as carers?

Child-welfare services, whether formal or informal, have had little success so far in

68

engaging with men, even though these services are potentially important sources of support, especially but not exclusively to fathers in what might be termed 'vulnerable' categories: unemployed fathers, young fathers, non-resident fathers, and stepfathers. Drawing on the available research, this paper explores the main issues in relation primarily to men as users of services, although some crossover into issues for men as workers can also be identified. Such experience must of course be located within wider structural factors, raising key issues for the development of a more sensitive public-policy agenda.

At service level, the approach of workers to engaging with men is often ambivalent. Although workers may express a wish that men should be more active in the care of their children, and more supportive to their female partners, in practice they often provide services which are predominantly geared to addressing women's needs (except where they are dealing with lone fathers). And while it is true that men may absent themselves from responsibility for child-care, it is also true that they may be 'screened out' by such ambivalence.[4]

As a result, men are not only absent from discussions about the welfare of their children, but they are also absolved from responsibility. In turn, this places women under great pressure to take prime responsibility and be 'fit mothers'; meanwhile, workers routinely avoid assessing fathers by the same rigorous criteria, tending to see them in the role of 'supplementary' carer, rather than co-parent. Redressing this balance so that services put in place identifiable strategies to include men is a critical task for policy, training, and practice.

At the same time it is important to acknowledge that there are risks in involving men in child-care. Workers may rightly decide to avoid contact with a particular man, owing to the potential and/or actual extent of his violence or abuse towards his partner or children. There is also a related argument that the hidden and under-reported extent of male violence and abuse should place significant restrictions on the numbers of men employed as child-carers and the way in which they carry out their role.[5] These concerns are real, and protection issues must therefore be clearly addressed within services and agencies, so that safeguards are in place to minimise risks and ensure that proper training, supervision, and support are readily available. More broadly, if the culture of child-welfare institutions is based upon empowerment and openness, the potential for abuse will be minimised.

Another source of tension that inhibits male participation in services, either as users or workers, is that many women are wary that it may result in men taking over one of the few arenas — caring for children — in which women are able to exert some control over their lives. However, there is also the argument that perpetuation of the identification of women with children damages women's wider economic and social opportunities. If child-welfare services are to articulate gender roles positively, and thereby help to release women from being defined purely as the carers, they must engage with men more actively.

Nevertheless, this is a tension that must be managed constructively. At service level, it may be that female users (and sometimes male users) will want to address some issues separately in single-sex groups, and such wishes should be taken into account. Within organisations as a whole, the corollary to attempts to increase men's participation as workers should surely be encouragement for women to enter senior management positions.[6]

A final set of obstacles to male involvement are essentially practical. Long working hours or irregular employment patterns may preclude men's attendance at times when services are open. Services may also lack any 'father-friendly' orientation or 'feel'. For instance, the physical environment of posters, photographs, and information leaflets may not convey the message that men's participation is valued. The nature of the welcome given to male users may well affect their desire to come through the door again; although having male workers may be useful, there is no firm evidence that their presence is essential. Male attenders may also perceive the activities on offer as too 'passive', which leaves staff with the dilemma of how to attract men while seeking to challenge gender stereotypes.[7]

There are no easy solutions to this wide range of issues, and addressing and managing the tensions in engaging with men are primarily a matter of making gender visible within services. As the latest UK research argues,[8] it is vital to create opportunities for informed and on-going discussion and reflection among male and female workers and managers (and, where relevant, with service users of both sexes as well) in order to move forward on key matters of policy and practice. As with protection strategies, if this approach is to be successful, it requires consistent backing from the agencies within which such services are located.

Developing the public-policy agenda

Although it is perhaps easiest to effect positive change at service level, it is important to set what happens locally against the prevailing economic, social, and cultural background. How men and women think about caring for children, and how they act in practice are obviously closely linked to these broader issues. In the UK, current interest in men and fathers is the culmination of three decades of significant social change, and law and policy has yet to catch up. One recent overview of 21 studies of fatherhood in Britain[9] concluded that a gap exists between the complex reality of modern fatherhood that results from diversifying family and employment patterns, and the enduring and pervasive attitudes that link mothers to child-care and fathers to breadwinning.

In comparison with previous administrations, the current UK government's approach to men as carers appears relatively forward-looking. In general there is less focus on enforcing the financial responsibilities of 'feckless fathers' and conjuring up nostalgic images of the post-war nuclear family. Overall the discourse has been generally father-friendly. In policy terms, the legal rights of the unmarried father whose name is on a child's birth certificate are to be extended. There is the introduction of unpaid parental leave, paternity leave, and the right to work a 48-hour week. And a range of initiatives have been established to improve parenting and child-care which are likely to bring some benefits for fathers as well as mothers: a National Childcare Strategy; the 'Sure Start' Programme for children under four years of age; and a National Family and Parenting Institute.

However, this is only a partial picture. Although the rights of unmarried fathers are being extended, government statements still tend to value marriage over other family forms. Employees' parental leave and paternity leave is unpaid, and there are fears that in practice men will simply not use it.[10] Maybe it would be worth while to adopt the Scandinavian approach of reserving a certain portion of leave for the father which is lost if unused. And despite the recent child-care initiatives, pay and conditions remain very poor: a significant reason why men do not work in this field.

Beyond specific policy measures, on the cultural level one might have thought that the recent birth of the Prime Minister's son Leo would provide an excellent platform for an informed debate about the role of fathers, the importance of men taking paternity leave, and so on. This has not happened, although thanks to the British press we now know how to create a nursery aligned according to the dictates of *feng-shui*, or even a bomb-proof maternity room. Beyond trivia of this kind, we are still waiting in the UK for a serious discussion about what policy makers and service providers can do to encourage men to be carers. It is an enormous challenge, but one with significant potential to enhance gender equality in the twenty-first century.

Notes

1   N. Chodorow (1978), *The Reproduction of Mothering: Psychoanalysis and the Sociology of Gender*, University of California Press.

2   G. Russell (1983), *The Changing Role of Fathers*, Oxford University Press.

3   Findings from the National Child Development Study, cited in C. Lewis (2000), *A Man's Place in the Home: Fathers and Families in the UK*, Joseph Rowntree Foundation.

4   J. Edwards, 'Screening out men', in J. Popay, J. Hearn, and J. Edwards (1998), *Men, Gender Divisions and Welfare*, Routledge.

5   K. Pringle (1998), 'Men and childcare: policy and practice', in Popay et al., op. cit.

6   A. Burgess and S. Ruxton (1996), *Men and their Children: Proposals for Public Policy*, Institute for Public Policy Research, London.

7   D. Ghate, C. Shaw, and N. Hazel (2000), *Fathers and Family Centres*, Policy Research Bureau.

8   C. Cameron, P. Moss, and C. Owen (1999), *Men in the Nursery*, Paul Chapman Publishing.

9   C. Lewis, op. cit.

10   In December 2000, the UK government published a consultation paper that described options for positive reform, including the right to reduced working hours for all parents (but not paid parental leave).

'Sitting on a rock': men, socio-economic change, and development policy in Lesotho

Caroline Sweetman

From 1989 to 1992, I was involved in planning and running a UNICEF-sponsored development project in Lesotho, which aimed to promote gender equity through the pages of a women's magazine. While print journalism may seem a rather unlikely medium through which to contact grassroots women, this magazine was avidly and widely read: a sign of Lesotho's high female literacy rate, which in 1990 was estimated by the UNDP at 84 per cent. This figure looks even more remarkable in comparison with the male literacy rate of 62.2 per cent (UNDP 1990). The particular course taken by colonial and neo-colonial 'development' in Lesotho has made it, until recently, a rational choice for families to opt to educate their daughters rather than their sons.

For 150 years, since exports of grain from Lesotho were stemmed by British and South African economic policies (Murray 1981), teenage boys have travelled away from Lesotho to the mines of South Africa to begin a life of hardship and danger, both down the mines and in the migrant hostels (Ramphele 1993). The average Mosotho man spends 14 years — one-third of his working life — in the mines (*Shoeshoe* 1992). In contrast, women have been prevented from legally migrating to find work[1] through controls exerted by their spouses, chiefs, the colonial administration in Lesotho, and the pass laws of apartheid-era South Africa.

Migrant mining has meant a relatively high female participation rate in Lesotho's formal labour force,[2] whereas boys have not until recently needed an education to secure work in the mines. Money has, in consequence, been directed to female education. Many male children do not attend school, but work instead as *balisana* (herdboys). In 1980, mean years of schooling for girls were 3.0 years, compared with 2.4 years for boys (UNDP 1980: 129). In a 1990 Situation Analysis of conditions for women and children in Lesotho, UNICEF stated 'if there is only one boy in the family, he will probably never attend school' (UNICEF 1990: 129). Herdboys — some as young as four years old — have been the target of development

interventions by UNICEF, to educate them and ameliorate the harsh conditions of their existence (Thai, 1992, no page number).

However, this has all started to change. The process of mass retrenchments of Basotho men from the mines began in 1987 — although it is only now starting to attract widespread interest, because of the severe economic, political, and social implications for the country (McNeil 1998). The loss of the mining wage is having a huge impact, at both national and household levels. In 1988, mineworkers' remittances were roughly equal to gross output in the domestic economy: 97.7 per cent per cent of GDP (Cobbe 1991). Despite development funding being poured into Lesotho in order to stimulate agriculture as an alternative to mining, Lesotho's agricultural sector is moribund: population pressure means that by 2003, agriculture will produce only an estimated 22 per cent per cent of the maize required for domestic consumption (Gay 1993). Media reports associate family dislocation and escalating male violence with widespread unemployment for uneducated ex-miners.

In 1993, I began work at Oxfam GB as a gender adviser and researcher. The gender specialist team at head office, which I joined, focused their attentions on women. Suggestions that men might suffer through certain forms of gendered social relations led to comments such as: '*Why should we work with men? It would be like doing anti-poverty work and targeting the landlords!*' Yet how does one make sense of social relations in the case of Lesotho if one starts from the assumption that gender relations mean that women are always the losers? Increasingly, in contexts like Lesotho, working to further feminist goals makes it necessary to analyse men's participation in daily life and the sexual division of labour, and male gender identity. Mass redundancy of Basotho men from minework in South Africa is causing a crisis in intra-household relations, owing to unequal power relations between women and men, and men's inability to fulfil the role of family breadwinner. The outcome of this is crisis within ex-miners' households, including higher rates of violence against women. Change in gender relations as a result of redundancy clearly has a negative impact on both women and men, and of course on their dependants.

Crisis, gender, and violence against women

I undertook research in Lesotho in June 1993, shortly before joining Oxfam, into the ways in which gender relations were changing in 29 households where men had been made redundant from the mines in South Africa (Sweetman 1995). At that time, it was already possible to see that these redundancies would herald a significant economic crisis, at national and household levels. Numbers of Basotho mineworkers peaked in the South African mines in 1987, when 126,000 were employed.[3] From the 1987 miners' strike, which led to almost 4000 Basotho redundancies from the mines of South Africa,[4] to the time of my research in 1993, the issuing of contracts to Basotho miners working in South Africa fell dramatically. Numbers have continued to fall since then. At the time of my research, 25,000 miners, and the households linked to them through the chain of dependency, were threatened with post-retrenchment impoverishment. My study was an early attempt to examine the effect of such systemic crisis on 29 ex-migrant miners' households,[5] with regard to the sexual division of labour and gender relations.

I found in Lesotho that household realities may belie popular notions about which activities are performed by women, and which by men – a case argued also by Sarah White (White 1997). In Lesotho, rural livelihoods have, throughout the last century, depended largely (and increasingly, as a result of environmental degradation) on mining remittances. In 1988, such remittances were roughly equal to gross output in the domestic economy: 97.7 per cent of GDP. In contrast, Lesotho's agricultural sector is relatively moribund, earning 176.7 million maloti in 1988 (23.5 per cent of GDP) (Cobbe 1991: 22). When I asked women what they did each day when their husbands still had jobs in mining, I was prepared for accounts of overworked women with multiple livelihood strategies, but not for the response that actually I got. When I asked one respondent what activities she undertook in addition to child-care

and housework, she replied: '*Nothing – I just sit on a rock*'.

However, when I probed more deeply, 60 per cent of my respondents did admit that they had earned money while their husbands were employed in the mines. It seemed that Basotho women's productive activities – for example, the sale of crops from their gardens – were hidden; certainly from me as a researcher, and possibly from their husbands. They did not want to be seen to be contributing income to the household.[6] In marriages where couples spent long periods apart, maintaining a fiction of complete dependence on a male breadwinner seemed to smooth the path of marital relationships. Forty per cent of respondents had eschewed income generation altogether before retrenchment, in favour of obeying traditional bans on female income generation and remaining in the domestic sphere, respecting what Deniz Kandiyoti has termed the 'patriarchal bargain' – a rigid adherence to gender norms and the sexual division of labour: 'protection in exchange for submissiveness and propriety' (Kandiyoti 1988: 283). During mass male migrancy, ensuring sustained access to a regular mining remittance through observing gender stereotypes in this way may be argued to be a woman's best chance of well-being for herself and her children.

Of course, income generation is not totally precluded in all cases – in fact, some writers assert that during migrancy women have authority to choose income-generating activities (Palmer 1985). However, the ideological construction of these activities is as an extension to 'reproductive' subsistence agriculture, and is characterised by an emphasis on 'consumption rather than investment' (Sebsted and Grown 1989: 941). In line with this, gender analysis of women's livelihoods in many contexts world-wide has shown that, far from being an accurate depiction of women's lives, the assumption that women perform reproductive duties in the private sphere while men earn money in production in the public sphere masks a much more complex reality. In Africa, the 'domestication' of women into housewives was a part of the colonial project; African women had always played an active role in production (Hansen 1992). Feminist economists have argued that an association of women with reproduction and men with production is actually an effective means of depressing the cost of labour as part of the project of capital accumulation in the colonial and neo-colonial eras (Folbre 1994).

After redundancy, desperation on the part of Basotho women to ensure the survival of their families made women's work in the informal sector much more obvious than it had been previously. In contrast, there was only very limited re-employment of men, breaking the association of masculine identity with production. Among miners retrenched since 1991, only 33 per cent were working by mid-1993. The prime importance of the male wage has also gone: the average monthly wage was M282-55: 63 per cent less than average earnings in the mines. The generally low level of formal education among miners[7] limited the chances of ex-miners of finding construction and similar work demanding skills akin to those gained in minework. There was a predictable correlation between the length of unemployment and the likelihood of ex-miners finding work.

The sudden visibility of women's on-going productive work now that men were present in the household and often unemployed themselves shattered conventional notions about what women and men contributed to household livelihoods. It showed that the male : urban : production paradigm was an inaccurate ideological construct which had evolved out of economic and social necessity, rather than being a natural 'given'.

As the proportion of income brought into the household by wives rose, so did domestic violence. Fifty-three per cent of my respondents in Lesotho admitted to being beaten by their husbands, and all of them said that the violence was worse after redundancy. Violence against women is, in this case, an indicator not only of the new physical proximity of husbands and wives after the end of male migration, but of the impact on gender relations of the economic and social crisis of male redundancy. Women recognised this more readily than they recognised the injustice of violence against women. One respondent told me: *'He is frustrated because he is no longer working and gets fed-up for almost anything, to the extent of beating me for minor things. He is an unhappy man, you see, but he is basically good'* (Sweetman 1995: 36). Not all women said they disagreed with wife-beating; some said that it was acceptable for a man to beat his wife *'to correct a fault'*.[8] Violence against women within the household is rooted in beliefs that the female partner is junior, and (through the tradition of *lobola*, bride-price), the property of her husband.

Responses from gender and development practice

Neither my theoretical grounding in gender analysis, my personal feminist commitment, nor my knowledge of the work of development organisations was of help to me in negotiating the minefield of possible perspectives and policy responses that could be made in response to changing gender relations in Lesotho. While Gender and Development (GAD) has the potential to be a radical approach, many international and national development organisations (both inside and outside government) have taken a more conservative approach. GAD as applied by male-dominated bureaucracies retains many of the features of Women in Development (WID). Approaches most commonly used by development organisations, including Oxfam GB, can be characterised, using Caroline Moser's typology, as those of **efficiency** — focusing primarily on increasing women's participation in the public sphere to drive the development effort — and **welfare/anti-poverty** — providing women with practical solutions to enable them to continue to meet their heavy domestic responsibilities (Moser 1989). Promoting girls' education and women's role in production are both in line with this vision.

Girls' and boys' education

What does gender and development policy have to offer when considering boys' education in Lesotho? There is the problem of a 'forgotten generation' of male children, who herd animals rather than receive an education, and will grow up to find that unskilled jobs in mine-work no longer exist. What is the right policy solution to this? It is clearly a minority issue (albeit a critical one for every boy who is kept out of school in Lesotho): after all, two out of every three of the 110 million children out of school in developing countries are female (UNESCO 1996).

Gender-sensitive development policy on education in international and national development organisations tends to focus on the supply-side of the equation — i.e. the fact that there are simply too few education opportunities available to children in developing countries. Typical strategies include advocating more State spending on schools; or funding educational facilities where there is little or no State provision (for example, building schools, providing text books and stationery, and paying teachers' salaries). They also include supporting activities which deliberately aim to get more girls into school (ranging from providing transport and sanitary facilities at school for girls' use, to training teachers and education officials in gender awareness, and providing support to ensure that textbooks challenge gender stereotyping) (Stromquist 1994).

However, at the moment, it is the opposite question of getting boys into school that faces Lesotho's education system. The fact that all children have an inherent right to an education has provided a rationale for strategies such as the promotion of radio-based distance learning that is attractive to UNICEF in Lesotho (*Shoeshoe* 1992), but this has not been explicitly linked to a gender and development strategy (personal observation, 1992).

A way forward might be to focus more on the demand for education from parents. Gender and Development approaches to education have highlighted the (very real) issues of 'gender bias' and prejudice against girls' education *per se*, which means that many girls do not receive an education. However, the fact that it is boys in Lesotho who have not been sent to school suggests that deciding how to spend limited funds available for children's education is surely at least as much a *pragmatic* decision as one based on cultural norms. Parents have to consider the relative cost of education as against the likelihood of a child finding employment, and in most contexts this means educating boys. In the case of Lesotho, boys have not needed education to become breadwinners, so girls have benefited by default.

In line with this view that demand-side factors in choosing whether to educate girls or boys are at least as much motivated by pragmatism as based on prejudice, in my research 90 per cent of women respondents said that boys' education would become more important to them if there proved to be no future in mining. However, 82 per cent of respondents said they considered education to be important for girls and boys equally, and 16 per cent said they would continue to prefer to educate girls: 'Girls care for their parents more than boys do' (Sweetman 1995: 42). Perhaps parents should be given more credit for taking sensible decisions in an unjust world. Ultimately, strategies to increase children's education, and to ensure that both sexes get an equal chance of education, need to be seen in the context of broader economic and social

development which challenges conventional assumptions that men are breadwinners and women are dependent wives and mothers. Patterns of opportunity and employment are gendered. In Lesotho, now that the loss of the mining remittance has plunged entire households into economic crisis, funding any child's education is increasingly difficult. If efforts are made to get boys into school, there is a danger that girls will be taken out. In the short term, of course, it is critical to continue to challenge parents' perceptions that children of one or other sex are not worth — or do not need — educating.

In Lesotho, I talked to an international consultant employed by the World Bank to work with the Ministry of Education to develop a national educational strategy. She did not see any need to work with families whose sons faced a bleak future of unskilled work as children, followed by unemployment in adult life; she maintained that attitudes towards educating sons would gradually change, once parents realised that they needed to educate boys.[9]

Livelihoods, money, and violence against women

Development organisations seem to have focused the huge majority of their 'gender' interventions on integrating women into economic development outside the household, relying on slender evidence that in so doing they are 'empowering' women; yet focusing on women alone simply contributes to overload and exhaustion for women, in an era when the State can be relied upon even less than previously to provide social services (Folbre 1994). In addition, women may be placed at increased risk of male violence.

It is essential that any study of women's changing livelihoods should seen in the context of those of men. While the nature of men's and women's work is seen in many contexts as natural, 'traditional', and unchanging, economic and political circumstances oblige individuals to challenge or reinforce these norms continuously. Deniz Kandiyoti paraphrases Henrietta Moore when she observes: 'gender ideologies are not merely cultural beliefs and attitudes which are somehow attached to economic and political processes but are actually *constitutive* of them' (Kandiyoti, 1998).

What does the application of a gender analysis tell us about patterns of male and female income generation? In many industrial countries, opportunities for men to fulfil the role of sole economic provider, bringing in enough cash to support the nuclear family, are diminishing, as changing patterns of employment favour insecure, low-paid, part-time jobs for a female workforce. In the rapidly industrialising countries in the South, a trend similar to employing women in manufacturing and the service sector is occurring. As Patrice Engle (1997) notes, social-policy makers are currently addressing the issue of 'male exclusion' from formal employment. The media depict increasing numbers of female-headed households which receive no economic support from absent fathers, and social problems that are perceived as resulting from male unemployment, including escalating male violence in the family, and rising crime among young unemployed men and boys.

Shifting from a 'Women in Development' (WID) approach to a 'Gender and Development' (GAD) approach has stimulated a debate on how women's increased involvement in income generation affects women's status within the household. Yet there is relatively little work done to assess the nature of this link and its relation to the incidence of violence against women within marital relationships. Supporting women who have survived marital violence tends still to be seen as a task for women's organisations, rather than an essential part of development policy and practice: yet the cost of violence to women, their families and society is incalculable (Heise 1995), and is clearly an issue for all involved in development. In a context where men's role as provider for the family is under threat, it is quite clear that while bringing in more money to the household *may* increase women's ability to negotiate in the home, it may also have the result of triggering increased violence within the home. Women are not beaten because they have money, or because they lack it; rather, they are beaten by men who know that they are permitted by social norms to beat women, and who see violence as a method of reasserting their domination in the face of women's challenges to this fact (Kabeer 1998, in the context of credit programmes in Bangladesh).

The primary focus of most organisations — whether focused on development or women's rights — that work with women in the kind of situation that I encountered in Lesotho tends to be on ensuring that women have economic independence, which would logically mean that they could leave violent men. This is obviously very good news. However, listening to women in Lesotho who wanted to leave their husbands, it was clear that, even if they felt able to do so on economic grounds, they would not leave, because they could not take with them their children — who were seen as 'the children of the house' — without immense courage to defy community norms (Sweetman 1995: 36). If women are to live with men and weather changes in economic and social participation safely, development must promote changes in male gender identity, through making connections between versions of hegemonic masculinity, the socialisation of young boys, and structural violence (Large 1997). We need a social policy that respects the need — and wish — of most women to live alongside men in their private lives as well as outside the house, free of the fear of violence.

What kinds of policy do we need?

What transformatory development policy and practice could result from focusing properly on the links between changing patterns of men's and women's work, challenges to gender norms, and the impact of these forces on poverty and social stability? This section will briefly consider a few of the implications that spring to mind.

The example of Lesotho shows us that it would not be desirable to focus on men alone in development interventions intended to support ex-miners' families, any more than the focus should remain exclusively on women. A focus on men would require policy makers to jettison all the progress made in Lesotho on educating women, and attempt to reverse what is essentially a very positive trend towards ensuring female education and literacy. Similarly, a focus on promoting men's employment in Lesotho upon redundancy from migrant work would be to disempower women who have worked in income generation – albeit tacitly in many cases — while their husbands were absent from home.

Interventions should, instead, focus on the household from a gender perspective, and contain components which address both women's and men's need to be able to undertake activities that are essential for household survival and stability, regardless of conventional assumptions about women's and men's work.

This would demand attention to raising awareness about the way in which conventional notions of women's and men's roles differ from reality; and about the ways in which aspiring to match such stereotypes holds back both men and women from attaining peace and prosperity. Key to this approach would be the idea that 'the prosperity of the household depends on the totality of various activities' (Sen 1987: 12). One respondent in my Lesotho research, whose husband had been out of mining work for 14 years, stood out as having a stable household-livelihood strategy with a number of interacting elements: close co-operation between herself and her husband, a strong entrepreneurial spirit, flexibility in budgeting, a strong female input into decision making, and absence of marital violence. Productive and reproductive strategies were combined in the interests of surviving retrenchment, and the marital partners appeared to be relatively unhampered by the former ideological polarisation of gender roles. Development interventions need to help, rather than hinder, such a holistic solution to household and marital crisis.

In particular, men's and boys' existing roles in the family need to be emphasised, and these roles strengthened or challenged as appropriate. A first step in this process would be to give more attention to analysing men's livelihood activities in a way similar to the manner in which women's are analysed. Frameworks such as that of Sebsted and Grown (1989) depict women as individuals with dependants whose well-being is intimately connected to their own.

Recognising the value of men's role as providers

Not only right-wing media commentators, but a wide range of people — including some GAD practitioners in development organisations — are currently responding to changing patterns of male and female employment, and rising numbers of female-headed households, by condemning men for failing in their socially ascribed role of 'provider'. In development organisations, this attitude has led to the deterministic stereotyping of men in Northern and Southern countries as feckless, irresponsible, and ultimately incapable of change. As Sarah White observes, 'Good girl/bad boy stereotypes present women as resourceful and caring mothers, with men as relatively autonomous individualists, putting their own desires for drink or cigarettes before the family's needs' (White 1997: 16).

In common with all such uncritical assumptions, the notion of feckless men conceals a complex reality, in which some men are victims, as well as women and children. Gender analysis suggests that the processes known as 'male exclusion' and the 'feminisation of labour' are part of the continuing process of industrial development along capitalist lines; as in Lesotho during the era of mass male migration, ideas about what constitutes 'women's work' and 'men's work' continue to be manipulated to depress the cost of production still further. Necessity sends Basotho men to the mines to earn a 'family wage': in the era of mining, households with an income from the mines were reckoned by Walhstrom to have an income 'much above the average' (Wahlstrom 1990: 6). Miners lived in appalling conditions in the hostels in South Africa (Ramphele 1993), facing dangers each day in mines where safety conditions were lax. Such a livelihood demands extreme bravery. On redundancy, ex-miners are faced with a crisis in their ideas of what it means to be a man. Once these ideas cease to fit the external world in which they operate, alienation or an 'identity crisis' is likely to result. Margrethe Silberschmidt discusses this and links it to mental illness in her paper on the Kisili community in Kenya (Silberschmidt 1991).

Patrice Engle (1997) has looked at the role of fatherhood in three dimensions. This 'triple role' is that of biological father, economic provider, and 'social father'. In common with more familiar analytical frameworks used by gender and development policy makers and practitioners — for example, Caroline Moser's concept of women's 'triple role' (Moser 1989) — Engle's use of the three roles emphasises how the involvement of parents (who may not have to be male, except in the case of biological fatherhood!), in both public and private spheres, is critical for family survival and stability. However, the way in which fatherhood is experienced by individual men varies according to precedents and traditions set by wider society, to current social and economic conditions, and to the dynamics of particular families and the individuals within them. In Lesotho, fatherhood demands that a man is absent from his household and working in the mines, to earn income. Patrice Engle asserts that, while male fertility is a defining aspect of male identity across all cultures, and the role of 'provider' is also seen as important in most societies (even while individual men may in actuality reject this responsibility), being a 'social father' in the sense of meeting the day-to-day demands of caring for children is less commonly seen as an essential part of the male role, even while many men may take on more of this role as children mature.

Challenging ideas of who does unpaid domestic work

The Lesotho case belies the belief that most unpaid family work is done by women: this is clearly at odds with the reality of herd-boys' work. However, evidence from around the world indicates that the vast majority of unpaid work within the home continues to be done by women, despite difficulties in defining and counting this work (Whitehead 1999).

Development interventions, even when termed 'gender-sensitive', have not tended to pose a direct challenge to the idea that domestic chores and the role of day-to-day caring for the family must necessarily be carried out by women and girls. Instead, interventions have commonly sought to reduce the time and energy that women expend in activities such as collecting fuel and water. This kind of intervention has evolved as a response to a critique of approaches which seek to involve women in increased income generation and other production — recognising that, if this is not linked to attempts to diminish the time women spend on reproductive work, the result will be simply to overburden them. Yet the limited success of such projects means that women's workloads often increase nonetheless, and unpaid reproductive work may be taken on by other women, often older women or daughters.

Just as the association of men with production needs to be challenged, so too does the assumption that domestic work cannot be taken over by men. Of course, the question remains as to how the necessary shift in attitudes to domestic work can take place, given the iterative, complex, and context-specific nature of the link between the work as a signifier of gender, the gender-specific valuing of the work, and the status ascribed to the sex of the person who performs it. This is obviously an extremely difficult issue. Moreover, not only is doing 'women's work' unacceptable to many men, but women themselves may be unwilling to allow part of their role to be taken over by their partners (Engle and Leonard 1995). Women

may be resistant to men taking over the most symbolically female parts of their work. As Sarah White points out (1997), gender concerns not only persons, but values. She quotes Bob Connell, stating: 'masculinity is shaped in relation to an overall structure of power (the subordination of women to men) and in relation to a general symbolisation of difference (the opposition of femininity to masculinity)'. Doing different work is a key part of this process of rendering women and men 'different' from each other. Chenjerai Shire illustrates this point in his research into the symbolic significance of men's and women's work tools, and the connection between these and feelings of maleness and femaleness, in another Southern African context: a Shona community in Zimbabwe (Shire 1994).

Rejecting prejudices about 'lazy men'

Development policy should be based on a commitment to involving both sexes in development interventions, with no prejudices about over-estimating or under-estimating women's or men's commitment to work. Prejudices about 'lazy men' in areas of Southern Africa where there is mass male migration stem from a combination of prejudice and flawed research methodology (Whitehead 1999).

If men are resistant to particular kinds of intervention, we should be asking why. In general, as discussed earlier, gender analysis in development has focused on promoting women's participation in different arenas, and also focuses on the gaps in their participation, asking why this is. Where women themselves are resistant to the idea of undertaking new activities — for example, taking part in credit schemes — extension workers discuss their reservations, which are listened to carefully. In comparison, as Gisela Geisler has noted (1993) in the context of agricultural projects in Southern Africa, men's resistance to participating in development interventions is simply worked around. The inactivity of men who sit under trees is acknowledged and laughed at, and then the women's project gets underway.

Implications for resourcing the new agenda

Finally, it should be pointed out very plainly that there are serious implications for feminists of taking on a concern for male gender identity and the need to work with men to change attitudes and behaviour. Feminists in development organisations, including myself, faced with the continuing overwhelming evidence of women's global economic, political, and social marginalisation, have opted to use our scant resources in working with women, to redress the enormous imbalance in gendered control over resources world-wide. Many opponents of the idea of working on men and masculinity see the option of debating male gender identity and targeting initiatives at men as well as women as, at best, a distraction in the face of the priority of focusing on women; and, at worst, as a part of an anti-feminist 'backlash'. As Jeff Hearn states, there is a danger that 'the concept [of masculinity] may divert attention from women and gendered power relations' (Hearn 1996).

The anxiety on the part of some feminists in organisations over whether working on men and masculinity is part of the anti-feminist backlash can be closely linked to a very real fear over resourcing the new agenda: resources for gender and development work are tightly stretched in organisations, including Oxfam GB. As Pringle puts it, '[we] must carefully scrutinise where the financial support and personnel are coming from when men's services are established, and not rob potential or existing provision from other service users' (Pringle 1995:167). Development policy-makers, in academia as well as in development organisations like Oxfam, need to be clear about their reasons for focusing on men and male gender issues, ensuring that this work is seen as essential additional work on gender — which is both the most efficient and the most potentially empowering way forward for both women and men in a community. It is not work that diverts resources away from addressing the interests of women.

Notes

1　Although many have, in fact, travelled for illegal migrant work (Johnston 1997).
2　Female workforce participation rate in 1985/6 was 37.1 per cent , compared with an overall rate of 55 per cent (Bureau of Statistics, Maseru, 1992). In the civil service, 60 per cent of employees are female (Safilios-Rothschild 1976), although there is a 'glass ceiling' at Director level which is not evident from the statistics (personal observation 1992).

3　Central Bank: Annual Statistical Bulletin, quoted in Country Profile, 1989/90, p. 41, London: Economist Intelligence Unit.
4　Figures from the Employment Bureau of Africa (TEBA). Average Basotho complement on TEBA mines in 1987 = 108,895; in 1988 = 105,000 (Maseru: TEBA, 19 May 1993).
5　In the current study, members of the household were defined as 'anyone who regularly makes a financial contribution to the household, and anyone who is always present in the household'.
6　Future research is needed in contexts like this to explore the extent to which this kind of masking happens consciously. These questions are raised in Deniz Kandyoti's paper on the patriarchal bargain revisited (1998), which queries the extent of the capacity of disadvantaged groups to achieve a degree of articulation of their interests and to acquire the means to act in their furtherance.
7　Interview, Neil Rae, TEBA, Maseru, December 1991.
8　Interview, Tholoana Moruthoane, Law Office, Maseru, November 1990.

References

Cobbe, J. (1991) Lesotho: 'What will happen after apartheid goes?' Africa Today, first quarter, 1991

Engle, P. (1997) 'The role of men in families: achieving gender equity and supporting children', Gender and Development 5/2

Engle, P. and A. Leonard (1995) 'Fathers as parenting partners', in Families in Focus: New Perspectives on Mothers, Fathers andChildren, ed. J. Bruce, C.B. Lloyd, and A. Leonard, New York: Population Council

Folbre, N. (1994) Who Pays for the Kids? Gender and the Structures of Constraint, London: Routledge

Gay, John (1993) 'Lesotho in the Year 2001', unpublished, Maseru

Geisler, G. (1993) 'Silences speak louder than claims: gender, household and agricultural development in Southern Africa', World Development 21/2

Hansen, K. (1992) African Encounters with Domesticity, Rutgers University Press

Hearn, J. (1996) 'A critique of the concept of masculinity/masculinities' in M. Mac An Ghaill, *Understanding Masculinities,* Milton Keynes: Open University Press

Heise, L. (1995) 'Overcoming violence: a background on violence against women as an obstacle to development' in G. Reardon (ed.) *Power and Process,* Oxfam: Oxford

Johnston, D. (1997) 'Migration and Poverty in Lesotho: a Case Study of Female Farm Labourers', unpublished PhD thesis, London: SOAS

Kabeer, N. (1998) *'Money Can't Buy Me Love'? Re-evaluating Gender, Credit and Empowerment in Rural Bangladesh,* IDS Discussion Paper 363, University of Sussex

Kandiyoti, D. (1998) 'Bargaining with patriarchy', *Gender and Society* 2/3

Kandiyoti, D. (1988) 'Gender, power and contestation: "rethinking bargaining with patriarchy"', in C. Jackson and R. Pearson (eds.), *Feminist Visions of Development: Gender Analysis and Policy,* London: Routledge

Large, J. (1997) 'Disintegration conflicts and the restructuring of masculinity', *Gender and Development* 5/2

Lovett, M. (1990)'Gender relations, class formation and the colonial state in Africa' in *Women and the State in Africa,* ed. J. Parpart and K. Staudt, Lynne Reiner Publishers

McNeil, D. (1998) 'For the out-of-work miners of Lesotho, gold retains precious little lustre', *International Herald Tribune,* 17 June 1998

Moser, C. (1998) 'Gender planning in the Third World: meeting practical and strategic needs', *World Development* 17/11

Murray, C. (1981) *Families Divided: the Impact of Migrant Labour in Lesotho,* Cambridge: Cambridge University Press

Ramphele, M. (1993) *A Bed Called Home: Life in the Migrant Labour Hostels of Cape Town,* Edinburgh: Edinburgh University Press

Pringle, K (1995) *Men, Masculinities and Social Welfare,* UCL Press

Sebsted, J. and C. Grown (1989) 'Towards a wider perspective on women's employment', *World Development* 17/7

Sen, A. (1987) *Gender and Co-operative Conflicts,* WIDER

Shire, C. (1994) 'Men don't go to the moon: language, space and masculinities' in A. Cornwall and N. Lindisfarne (eds.) *Dislocating Masculinities: Comparative Ethnographies,* London: Routledge

Shoeshoe (1992) 2/1, periodical, Ministry of Information and Broadcasting, Lesotho

Silberschmidt, M. (1991) *Rethinking Men and Gender Relations,* CDR Research Report 16, Copenhagen: CDR

Stromquist, N. (1994) *Gender and Basic Education in International Development Co-operation,* UNICEF Staff Working Paper No.13

Sweetman, C. (1995) *The Miners Return: Changing Gender Relations in Lesotho's Ex-migrants' Families,* No.9, Gender Analysis in Development Series, University of East Anglia

Thai, B. (1992) 'Neglected children', *Shoeshoe,* 2/5, January 1992, Ministry of Information and Broadcasting, Maseru, Lesotho

Wahlstrom, A. (1990) *Lesotho: a Gender Analysis,* Lesotho: SIDA

White, S. (1994) 'Making men an issue: gender planning for "the other half"' in *Gender Planning in Development Agencies: Meeting the Challenge,* Oxford: Oxfam

White, S. (1997) 'Men, masculinities, and the politics of development', *Gender and Development* 5/2

Whitehead, A. (1999) '"Lazy men", time-use, and rural development in Zambia', *Gender and Development* 7/3

UNDP (1980) *Human Development Report,* Oxford: Oxford University Press

UNDP (1990) *Human Development Report,* Oxford: Oxford University Press

UNICEF (1990) 'Situation Analysis of Women and Children in Lesotho, Maseru'

About the contributors

Kamla Bhasin is a gender consultant and trainer, and co-ordinator of the NGO South Asia Programme of the Food and Agriculture Organization (FAO).
Postal address: 55 Max Mueller Marg, New Delhi, 1110 003, India.
E-mail: k.bhasin@vsnl.com

Anne Coles is a research associate at Queen Elizabeth House, University of Oxford. She was formerly a senior social-development adviser in the UKDepartment for International Development and she represented the UK at the DAC Working Party on Gender Equality from 1993 to1999.
Postal address: Kelham, Dock lane, Beaulieu, Hampshire, SO42 7YH, Great Britain.
E-mail:JohnandAnneColes@compuserve.com

Ben Fawcett is the Co-ordinator of the Engineering for Development Programme of the Institute of Irrigation and Development Studies at the University of Southampton, Southampton SO17 1BJ, Great Britain.
E-mail: bnf@soton.ac.uk

Feleke Tadele is a project co-ordinator for CARE in Georgia, and former social-development adviser with Oxfam GB in Ethiopia.
Postal address: CARE International in the Caucasus, 100 t. Tabidze Street, Tbilisi, 380062, Georgia. E-mail: Feleke_Tadele@care.org.ge

Milton Obote Joshua is a gender trainer, and lecturer at the Centre for Women's Studies and Gender Analysis, Egerton University, Kenya.
Postal address: PO Box 536, Njoro, Kenya.
E-mail: objdydpr@net2000ke.com

Shibesh Regmi is the Nepal Country Director for ActionAid.
Postal address: ActionAid Nepal, PO Box 6257, Kathmandu, Nepal.
E-mail: info@newera.wlink.com.np

Chris Roche is a senior policy adviser with Oxfam GB.
Postal address: Policy Department, Oxfam GB, 274 Banbury Road, Oxford OX2 7DZ, Great Britain. E-mail: croche@oxfam.org.uk

Sandy Ruxton is a regional policy adviser for Oxfam GB.
Postal address: Policy Department, Oxfam GB, 274 Banbury Road, Oxford OX2 7DZ, Great Britain. E-mail: sruxton@oxfam.org.uk

Sue Smith is a policy adviser in Oxfam GB's UK Poverty Programme.
Postal address: Policy Department, Oxfam GB, 274 Banbury Road, Oxford OX2 7DZ, Great Britain. E-mail: ssmith@oxfam.org.uk

Peter Sternberg is a development worker employed by ICD/CIIR. He has worked with CISAS as a health educator and researcher for four years.
Postal address: CISAS, Apartado Postal 3267, Managua, Nicaragua. E-mail: pms@ibw.com.ni

Caroline Sweetman is Editor of *Gender and Development* and a policy adviser for Oxfam GB.
Postal address: Policy Department, Oxfam GB, 274 Banbury Road, Oxford OX2 7DZ, Great Britain. E-mail: csweetman@oxfam.org.uk

Nadia Wassef is a researcher and member of the Egyptian Female Genital Mutilation Task Force.
Postal address: 10 Hale House, 34 Devere Gardens, Kensington, London W8 5AQ, Great Britain. E-mail: nrwassef@yahoo.co.uk